Haitian Coffee Grows on Trees

Tate Watkins

Cover art and interior drawing by Chris Koelle.

CONTENTS

1

INTRODUCTION

COFFEE GROWS ON TREES

FOR A COUPLE of years I thought that the semi-wild, half-forgotten coffee I'd seen growing in the mountains across Haiti was a recent development. In some places, small mountain houses are dwarfed by 60-year-old coffee trees that produce literally two cherries. And in Haiti, the joke is that if a tree still gives a single cherry, a farmer will not touch it with a machete to prune it, lest he lose the income that single cherry represents, minuscule as it may be. So he leaves it for another year, withering like a nursing home patient who's been forgotten in the corner of the game room and missed a week of meals.

One of the first Haitian coffee farmers I talked to said he could describe the past 30 years of the sector with one word: "negligence." But neglecting coffee in Haiti is anything but new. "A person must be somewhat conversant with travelling in Hayti," wrote James Franklin, a British "man of commerce" who visited the island several times in the 1820s, "before he can discover on his road that a coffee plantation is near him." Franklin was visiting a plantation in the mountains above a town called Léogâne, just west of the capital, which was the epicenter of the 2010 earthquake that decimated much of the country. He described it as "a very good illustration of the coffee settlements in general, all of which exhibit negligence…" He wouldn't even have recognized a coffee tree, he said, "growing as it did in a pyramidal form, surrounded by numberless other shrubs," but for the few red cherries he spotted on a lower branch of one plant. "I alighted from my mule to examine some trees just round the spot: as nearly as I could ascertain, every tree must have exceeded twelve feet in height, and I am convinced that each of them at the time would not have produced two pounds of coffee in the husk."[1]

In Haiti, coffee grows on trees. Technically, all coffee grows on trees. The brown beans that go into making your morning cup are actually the dried and roasted seeds of a tropical tree fruit. Once a year small red fruits, called cherries, develop on the branches. Inside each cherry are two seeds, or beans. In contrast to Haiti's farms, intensively managed coffee farms found across much of Central and South America keep trees cut back to a manageable height—more like shrubs. This channels the nutrients and energy plants gather from the sun and soil toward producing beans, which make money, instead of wasting resources sprouting too many woody trunks and branches. As most coffee is harvested by hand, keeping trees short also means that come harvest time pickers can easily reach the fruits.

It's not out of the ordinary to find 20-foot-tall coffee trees in Haiti. Few farmers have bothered to replant for a generation, and some have given up the crop altogether. Every farmer may not cut down all their coffee trees, but many of them will never take time and energy away from food crops to bother tending the small coffee groves that their fathers planted out back. That's one reason the average yield in Haiti is now just a third of the Central American average.[2]

If you visit Guatemala, representative of many better-developed coffee countries, you'll see mills that prepare more coffee for export in a week than Haiti does in a year. You'll also see a cutting-edge coffee laboratory at the four-story headquarters of the National Coffee Association, whose annual budget has recently hovered somewhere between $6 million and $11 million, funded by a 1 percent levy on exports.[3]

At the other end of the spectrum, Haiti's Ministry of Agriculture can't definitively say how many coffee farmers the country has. One of the most recent reports by its National Coffee Institute noted that government studies have mindlessly reproduced the same figure since 1983: Haiti has 200,000 coffee farmers. Over the 30-plus years and countless coffee reports since then, coups d'etat overthrew multiple governments, a handful of natural disasters devastated the country, an international embargo undercut the economy, population nearly doubled, and coffee production fell by half. "Thirty years later," the latest report reads, in French, "it is difficult to accept that these figures have not changed one iota." In the next sentence it quotes the "very approximate" 200,000-coffee-producers figure anyway.[4]

It may seem bizarre, but after living in Haiti for a few years, the underdevelopment of the coffee sector and its 20-foot trees began to make sense. The coffee sector isn't really about coffee, at least not entirely. Like much of what goes on in the country, it's often as much about marketing to aid groups or charities as it is about economic activity. It makes perfect sense if you can make as much or more through temporary aid funding than through productive endeavors. Setting up a coffee cooperative can become as much about chasing grant money, or securing the pickup trucks or solar panels or water filters that might come along with it, as it is about trying to run a viable enterprise that produces excellent coffee year after year.

And coffee isn't a special case—what happens in the sector is just a byproduct of the wider Haiti context. The political and economic foundations of the country aren't really set up to help common people prosper. But while that fundamental structure makes life difficult for many citizens, small changes on the margins have the potential to add up to real improvement for ordinary Haitians. And for those who live in the country's mountainous rural areas, coffee may provide an avenue to that sort of improvement.

The majority of Haitians are farmers, and for the foreseeable future agriculture will remain the default economic backbone of the roughly 6 million people who live in rural districts.[5] In addition to coffee, two other significant cash crops for Haiti's farmers are cacao, the raw ingredient for chocolate, and mangoes. Like coffee, cacao grows in mountains, but at lower altitudes. Mangoes grow across the country, but some of the best production areas—especially for the sweet Françique variety that accounts for most high-value exports—are in the flatlands of the Artibonite and Plateau Central regions. My first foray into the coffee sector was with TechnoServe, an organization that works with farmers in about two dozen tropical countries and is known for its coffee expertise; one of the group's biggest efforts in Haiti, however, involves helping rural farmers get organic mangoes to Whole Foods stores every spring.

After living in Haiti for a few years writing about economic recovery following the 2010 earthquake, TechnoServe hired me to research the country's entire coffee sector. That led me to decide to spend another year helping set up the Haiti Coffee Academy, a venture that works with small-scale farmers in the southeastern mountains. One impetus for the initiative is because in economic terms, coffee is known as one of the best cash crops for a tropical farmer, especially one with a small plot of land who has few resources beyond hand tools, organic fertilizers, and sweat. I remember a TechnoServe claim, that with just one-third of a hectare planted in coffee, about 0.80 acres, a smallholder in East Africa could be profitable. But there are plenty of challenges, which is why so many Haitian farmers have chosen to neglect or abandon coffee over the years.

If there comes a day that coffee no longer works for a Haitian farmer, then it only makes sense for him or her to turn to the next-best option, whether growing another crop, migrating to the city to look for work in a factory, or any other better opportunity. But for small-scale farmers in the mountainous areas across the tropics, coffee will likely remain an attractive option for two reasons: it can be profitable at such small scale, and global demand for quality coffee is skyrocketing.

Franklin, the 1820s visitor, noted that the coffee plantations he was used to seeing on British colonial islands were laid out neatly and precisely. "In Hayti," he wrote, "the scene is different: what is denominated there a coffee plantation, is neither more nor less than a large tract of land, throughout which grows spontaneously the coffee tree; not planted there by the people, but sprung from the seed which has fallen from those planted by the French and which escaped destruction during the revolution."[6]

When it comes to those tall and neglected trees, little seems to have changed in 200 years. Most Haitian farmers pay little attention to their coffee plants, which still stretch to towering heights. And they have some very good reasons for it, as I understood more and more over time.

A MODEST LUXURY

The way Americans drink coffee has transformed in recent years. There's a good chance that you've noticed the change even if you're not a coffee drinker. Seemingly normal people line up on streets outside cafes in places like San Francisco, Manhattan, and Portland, patiently waiting for espressos and pour-overs and not batting an eye when the tab is as high as the price of a newsstand magazine. At many of these shops baristas use digital scales to make sure the dosages of coffee and water are just right, preparing each brew by hand and with exacting detail, one serving at a time. Many of their customers drink coffee because they like the taste of coffee, as opposed to, say, drinking it as a vehicle for milk and sugar, or as a socially acceptable alternative to freebasing caffeine.

These taste-centric coffee nerds have become a lot like wine nerds. They really care about the country, region, or even farm where their coffee was grown. Some customers want to know about the agricultural and socio-economic conditions of where the coffee grew, as shown by the rise of programs like certified-organic and fair trade. Then come the real geeks—the people interested in the variety of the coffee plant, the altitude of the plantation, and how the beans were processed, all of which can influence how it tastes in the cup. And there's a lot of overlap among these groups. After all, the people who care most about how their coffee tastes are most likely to care about how the person who grew it was treated. And they'll probably also be willing to pay more for it.

In contrast to a vacuum-sealed tin can of pre-ground coffee from the grocery store, coffee sold to these fanatics often retails for $12 to $20 a bag and might come straight from a local roaster. Much of it is "single-origin," meaning that instead of being blended with different coffees from all over a country or the world, the beans come from either the same farm or a group of farmers from the same community. The bag label features the country of origin, if not the name of the farmer or cooperative group who grew it. Coffee used to be simply a commodity—any one bean was more or less interchangeable with another from anywhere else around the world. Today it's become much more.

The industry's fascination with origin leads to a lot of those comparisons with wine, which has an appellation system to label where the grapes that went into a particular vintage came from. Both coffee and wine are agricultural products with consumers who obsess over their origins. Both stress the subtleties of the plants' growing conditions and microclimates. And both focus on the importance of tasting—or cupping, as it's called with coffee—to evaluate quality. Professionals frequently cup an assortment of coffees side-by-side to compare quality and suss out the flavor notes that show through in different beans. Those flavors can be as diverse as blueberries, brown sugar, and bergamot. All the soil, climatic, and environmental conditions surrounding a coffee's cultivation—what French people and the wine industry call *terroir*—can influence that taste.

The comparisons between coffee and wine are probably spot on when it comes to drinking culture. But when it comes to the evolution of the U.S. market, a better comparison might be the rise of craft beer.

For about 50 years after Prohibition ended in 1933, beer was just beer—a yellow, fizzy, corn- or rice-based beverage that tasted watery and got you buzzed. A decade before the ban on alcohol, small breweries across the United States had made distinct styles of beer and served their local communities. Once alcohol was again made legal, big breweries were best-poised to ramp up production and meet the huge demand for beer. Their brewing and marketing strategies were identical— appeal to the masses with a lowest-common-denominator product—and they maximized profits with volume instead of striving for quality or differentiation. Beer became a bland, uniform beverage, and abundant and cheap corn and rice from America's grain basket provided perfect ingredients.[7]

In 1978, Congress legalized homebrewing, which had remained forbidden even after the 21st Amendment repealed Prohibition. In the coming years, a new generation of DIY brewers flourished, eventually transforming the industry. Their mission was basically to make good beer that they'd like to drink in their own homes and with their own friends. The craft forerunners used high-quality grains and aromatic hops in their recipes, experimented with weird ingredients, and produced an endless assortment of beers—sours, wheat beers, IPAs, fruit beers, stouts, honey beers, and many, many more. A lot of homebrewers went on to start small breweries, and their ethos opened up a new world of choice and quality for customers.[8]

In 2000, craft beer's volume was still just 2 percent of the market. Today, one in every 10 beers sold in the country is a craft, and in dollar terms, craft accounts for almost 20 percent of the value of all American beer. And even though the fizzy-yellow, lite beer market is currently shrinking, the craft segment continues to expand each year.[9]

The American coffee market has a similar story, especially its recent history. Today, the lower-quality segment of the coffee market—the tin cans that lined the pantries of my grandparents' generation—has completely stagnated at zero growth. In stark contrast, the specialty coffee sector—the high-quality, pricier segment of the market that's something akin to craft beer—has been exploding, growing by an estimated 10 percent annually for the past 15 years. Now, one out of every two coffees drunk in the United States is a specialty coffee.[10]

Like with craft beer, the boom has brought amazing diversity—from coffees that look more like tea and give off citrusy flavors, to coffees that taste almost chocolatey and have the consistency of whole milk, to everything in between. If you enjoy coffee and are interested in going full nerd, find a cupping to attend at a roastery in your area—many have regular public tastings. I never realized what coffee could be, or the wide and interesting range of flavors it could have, until I tasted six coffees from six different countries back-to-back. That diversity is on show in upscale cafes today, and not just in big cities on the coasts. Burgeoning coffee cultures in smaller towns like Chattanooga, Oklahoma City, and Louisville attest to the sea change. But for a long time, coffee was just coffee—a dark, sludgy beverage that tasted burnt and got you buzzed.

As Mark Pendergrast explains in his coffee history for the layreader, *Uncommon Grounds,* early-20th-century housewives roasted raw coffee beans in their homes across the country. Which is pretty much the same thing as saying that housewives across the country used to ruin coffee, because it's difficult to roast well or consistently on a stovetop. About a century ago Maxwell House and Folgers were two of the first companies to address that issue—they perfected roasting standardization, mass production, and distribution, putting a pot of coffee in every kitchen in America. The beans were bad by modern coffee-geek standards, but the roast quality was probably an improvement on many home roasts. It was also cheap, and it delivered caffeine—the only two criteria for many coffee drinkers both then and now. Coffee was all about market share—the national roasters that emerged in the coming decades fought for volume and competed mainly on price. U.S. consumption peaked in 1946, when every American drank an average of more than 2 cups per day, a level never reached again.[11]

U.S. COFFEE AVAILABILITY
(daily six-ounce cups per person)

Coffee availability, a proxy for consumption, peaked in 1946.[12]

In the 1960s, a Dutch immigrant named Alfred Peet started roasting his own coffee in the Bay Area. Peet had started at Hills Bros., a 20th-century coffee institution in San Francisco, and once on his own, he turned his attention to the particulars of the roast process. Instead of using the cheapest raw materials he could find, he bought high-quality beans, used dark roasts favored by Europeans, and insisted on selling his customers only freshly roasted coffee. In 1970, the three people who would go on to start Starbucks were drawn to Peet's coffee because of his focus on quality. Peet became their original supplier, and they traveled from Seattle to the Bay Area to apprentice under him, learning about his roasting techniques and coffee strategy. Largely thanks to Starbucks and its massive growth —the company now has about 13,000 U.S. locations—coffee started to become something more than a brand name on a tin can.[13] Customers focused increasingly on the beans inside—French Roast, Breakfast Blend, Dark Roast. Peet and Starbucks helped shift emphasis toward roasting methods and quality differentiation. Eventually, Starbucks added a large helping of milk- and espresso-based drinks. In the process they turned millions of Americans into coffee drinkers over recent decades.

Around the same time that Peet was getting his start, a Norwegian immigrant named Erna Knutsen was blazing her own path into the California coffee scene. She started as a secretary with an importer, fought her way into the cupping room, and carved out a niche paying high prices for great coffees from places like Indonesia, Ethiopia, and Yemen at a time when the rest of the industry was still obsessed with volume. It was Knutsen who coined the term "specialty coffees," in a 1974 interview with the *Tea & Coffee Trade Journal*. "There is an emerging group, largely young people…who value good coffee," she said in the interview, as relayed by Pendergrast in his book, "and I am certain that our end of the business will grow." She saw coffee evolving into one of "those modest luxuries," as she put it, "that most can still afford."[14] Once people like Knutsen started to seek out the best beans at the beginning of the supply chain rather than commodity-grade coffee bulked into shipping containers, there was a natural evolution at the end of the chain: lighter roasting.[15]

When you roast coffee, you're essentially cooking the dried, jade-colored coffee seeds—what's known as "green coffee." When you cook steaks, you probably cook them differently depending on the cut. Most people would take a filet off the grill long before they would a sirloin—the filet is better meat, as you can tell just by looking at the price tag. Cooking it rarer lets more of the natural beef flavor, and maybe even the grass the cow ate, shine through on the plate. But with the sirloin, you might not just cook it longer, you may even cover it with sautéed mushrooms or a thick sauce.

Roasting coffee is a similar concept, as George Howell explains. Howell opened a coffee roasting operation near Boston in 1975, where he focused on excellent quality and fresh roasts. He bought his beans from Knutsen. And if you're using the best beans, you don't want to cover up their inherent attributes, you want to let them come through in the cup. "The message starts to be, for single origin, you want to do a light roast…," Howell explains in the 2014 documentary *A Film About Coffee*, "…the awareness that dark roast covers things. It's like a heavy sauce."

People like Knutsen and Howell laid the foundation for today's coffee evangelists, who focus on quality, origin, and light roasts. Roasters like Stumptown, Counter Culture, and Intelligentsia were in the vanguard of this wave in the 1990s. Once this small segment of the industry shifted toward light roasts that accentuate where coffee beans come from, there was a natural corollary: doing due diligence to see for yourself exactly where those beans came from. A catch-all term developed to describe this practice: "direct trade."[16]

Direct trade has become a muddied descriptor, much in the way that George Orwell felt politicians and officials abused the word "democracy": everyone agrees that it sounds nice and evokes positive connotations, but it's been used by so many people to mean so many different things that it's lost much meaning. There is no industry-wide standard or official definition for direct trade. Many companies "certify" their coffees as direct-trade, which means that, in their eyes, it qualifies as such. But most coffee industry people would agree that direct trade boils down to transparency and traceability throughout the supply chain. And instead of having a third-party stamp your bag with a label like "fair trade" to signal that a product was produced responsibly, a company tries to directly show and tell its clientele how its product was produced.[17] The term is mostly used by smaller roasters—Starbucks, for instance, has its own set of so-called "C.A.F.E." standards that it holds itself to, which have to do with quality, financial transparency, and worker and environmental conditions.[18]

For Stumptown, a fundamental part of direct trade is buying "directly from the people who are making the coffee," instead of purchasing it in bulk on a commodity exchange. Counter Culture has specific criteria for a coffee to qualify as direct trade, which include visiting growers every couple of years, paying suppliers a relatively high export price for green coffee, and meeting a minimum quality threshold in cupping evaluations. Geoff Watts, a co-owner of Intelligentsia, describes direct trade partly by what it's not: "It's not a matter of flying in, taking pictures, filling out some forms, shaking hands and making some vague commitments." He goes on to describe direct trade as mutually beneficial, transparent, and about long-term relationships between coffee producers and buyers.[19]

A direct trade roaster sees for itself where beans come from, as opposed to simply calling up a coffee importer down the road or in another state and getting the story from them and them alone. Still, these roasters aren't flying back from the tropics with their coffee orders. Most roasters, even direct-trade pioneers, purchase most of their coffee from an importer that's based in the U.S., even if the roaster visited the farm and sat at the table hammering out the terms of purchase. It only makes sense—importers can specialize in the financing, logistics, and 12-month relationships that it take to move a product from tropical countries around the world to the American market. In practice, direct trade can be the difference between a buying relationship that goes only as far as the exporter in the capital city of a coffee growing country, whose owners maybe went to college in the United States or Europe and speak fluent English, and having a relationship down to the farm level. That may mean a single coffee farmer, or it might mean the management staff of a co-op of small growers in the remote hills of Colombia or Uganda.

Direct trade can definitely leave room for opportunistic behavior, a sort of coffee equivalent to green-washing, or slick-but-empty marketing. Releasing a pristine company report about how much you pay farmers for their coffee doesn't guarantee that you've actually paid them much more than they would have been paid anyway. Even for well-meaning companies and their customers, it can be difficult to figure out how much your purchases are helping the people at the beginning of the supply chain. Parts of the coffee chain are extremely fragmented, far-flung, and murky. Just posting the prices paid for green coffee, for instance, which some roasters do in a quest for transparency, doesn't necessarily give customers a good idea about how much of that price actually trickles down to farmers.[20]

A related trend borne out of direct trade is that it makes a lot of coffee people want to, as one industry professional put it to me, "play Indiana Jones," traveling to exotic locales and taking Instagram pictures of themselves beside ripe coffee cherry. One of the co-founders of La Colombe, a Haiti Coffee Academy supporter, is a pretty good example of this sentiment. On his Travel Channel reality show, "Dangerous Grounds," the gregarious founder comes off as a sort of MacGyver-meets-Mario Batali as a camera crew follows his exploits sourcing coffee around the world. I watched just one episode of the show, the Haiti one. In it, he plays up non-existent danger in a Port-au-Prince street market, talks about a guy called "the president" who supposedly doesn't let anyone buy coffee from his side of the mountain, and sleeps underneath his broken-down jeep because, he tells the audience, Haitians would steal it in the night if he didn't. It was pure fiction.

I asked one of our Haitian employees who does logistics and mechanical work what he thought of the final product. He speaks good English and had actually been the driver and fixer during the film shoot. "It was great!" he told me, laughing. He had loved the whole action-figure-hero ridiculousness of it all.

But what about the show's fabrications? Or the tropes about his country being nothing but a dangerous and dark place?

"It's a show," he said. "Everybody knows it's not real."

But it doesn't bother you that it's presented on TV as a true story, and to an audience who may know little about Haiti?

"No. It's just a show."

LET'S TALK COFFEE

Pierre Sanon looked to be at least 60 and wore black gumboots, a secondhand bomber jacket, and a toboggan hat—all par for the course for a Haitian farmer during the tropical winter. He had a question—he wanted to know about getting fertilizer, by which he meant chemical fertilizer, which the government subsidized and came into the country via importers in the capital. Sanon claimed that farmers needed chemical fertilizer to grow coffee properly, or to grow any other crop for that matter. Which is also par for the course when talking to a Haitian farmer.

I told him that chemical fertilizer can give really impressive and immediate results. But I also said that we weren't an aid group or NGO—a non-governmental organization, the charity and non-profit groups that often stumble over each other to work in the hot and sticky places around the world—and we weren't there to hand out fertilizer. It's possible to make fertilizer from kitchen waste, cow manure, and organic material, I said, and our farmer trainer would help him with every step of the process if he was interested. It would be nearly as good as any factory-made product, but it would take more labor and patience.

It was fall of 2014, and I was in my first few months of living in coffee country in southeastern Haiti working with growers. Cantave Fils-Aimé, an agronomist in a country that seems to have as many out-of-work agronomists as it does moto taxi drivers, was my co-manager. When Cantave and I weren't busy making sure the replanting of a 30-acre demonstration farm was going as planned, we were visiting small-scale farmers. Cantave's only child is his four-year-old daughter, and she and her education are his reasons for being, and for working. For him, coffee and his work represent a future for her.

On that November morning, we were visiting a group of 25 coffee growers in the mountains an hour or so above Thiotte, the regional town in that part of the country.[21] He and I lived there in a two-bedroom apartment attached to the one hotel that had 24-hour running water and electricity, thanks to solar panels. One of our three trainers had already been working with the farmer group for a few months, meeting every few weeks to go over different aspects of coffee growing. I gave a short talk about how we wanted to help them improve their coffee practices so that they could improve their livelihoods—maybe be able to send their kids to school, or at least earn enough income to be sure there was enough food to feed their families year round. That was the goal of the people backing the venture— the Clinton Foundation, which funds many do-good missions in Haiti and around the world. It had also enlisted La Colombe, a roaster in Philadelphia that had been buying coffee from the country for the past few years. That in itself was something, because there's not much Haitian coffee to go around these days, at least not compared to the past.

I always tried to keep my talks in Creole fairly short and then turn it over to Cantave. It's not just that he's Haitian and understands his language and culture infinitely better than I ever will. He also has a knack of talking to farmers in a way that's extremely relatable but at the same time not at all condescending. He comes from a very different socio-economic background than most smallholder farmers—he speaks perfect French and got his degree from a private university in Port-au-Prince. But he was originally from the countryside, the son of a farmer. He'd make cultural references or points about agriculture that resonated so perfectly with farmers that they'd invariably nod their heads and mutter approval. "Chemical fertilizer might seem like magic," he'd say. "You can see it working almost overnight. But what will you do when you can't find it one month, or when the price shoots up another month?" This had happened a handful of times in the past year—the Haitian government subsidized chemical fertilizer en masse and passed it on to selected middlemen, who then peddled it to farmers at a set price, taking their cut along the way. A few months prior, the main vendor in the region had hiked the price so much that people from neighboring villages blocked the road in protest. Cantave had told me that a group of villagers even torched a U.N. vehicle that tried to ignore their roadblock. "Too many farmers in this country *vin esklav angre chimik*"—become slaves to chemical fertilizer, he said. "If you can make your own, you don't have to rely on the government's supply, and you're better off."

Cantave always used a metaphor like that to make his point simply but perfectly. I would, on the other hand, revert to using the same tired Haitian proverb without fail, partly because I just really liked it, and partly because it seemed so apt for everything we were doing there: *Piti piti, zwazo fè nich li*—Little by little, the bird makes its nest.

One reason we wanted to help farmers increase their production was pretty straightforward: that way there would be more Haitian coffee to go around for U.S. buyers. You can hardly find Haitian coffee in an American cafe today, and for good reason. Since the 1980s, coffee production in the country has fallen by half, and exports have plummeted by 95 percent.[22] Well before that, the same tiny territory used to grow half the world's coffee. But that was a long time ago—before Haiti even became Haiti.

SMALL SCALE, BIG OPPORTUNITY

Roughly 50 countries produce coffee. Because frost kills the plant, temperature is the main factor that limits its growing range—to only the tropics. That's why, for Americans at least, there's no such thing as local coffee.[23] And even in the tropical belt of the globe, coffee is limited to the high-altitude, mountainous areas that have a particular temperature range and rainfall pattern. Most coffee plants also need about 50 percent shade and 50 percent sunlight.

The plant shares a botanical family with the gardenia flower, and while there are thousands of different species of coffee, only two are commercially significant: *arabica* and *canephora*. Generally speaking, the better the coffee plant does in the field, the worse it will taste in the cup. Arabica plants are delicate. They grow at high altitudes and give cups that are complex and bright. But the plants themselves are low-yielding and susceptible to disease. Canephora, on the other hand, can grow practically on the beach, is resistant to many pests and diseases, and gives roughly double arabica's yields. But it has a taste that's been described as something between sucking on burnt rubber and licking a hardwood floor. Canephora's vigor in the field has led to two things: its common name, robusta, and efforts to cross it with arabica in search of high-yielding but decent-tasting hybrids. Robusta's unpleasant taste means that it's relegated largely to instant coffee and low-grade blends. Partly because of the quality difference, arabica prices are routinely double robusta's on global markets where coffee is traded. If you're a discerning coffee drinker, then most of what you drink probably comes from arabica beans.[24]

There are about 20 notable arabica-producing countries, from Latin America to East Africa to the Asian Pacific. Coffee is native to just one, the highlands of Ethiopia, where people originally chewed the fruit as a stimulant. This wild Ethiopian coffee was later transported across the Red Sea to Yemen, the first place it was cultivated systematically. By the 1500s, people throughout the Muslim world were roasting, grinding, and brewing the beans. Arabians cherished their prospering industry, and in an effort to keep the market to themselves, they either boiled or parched all beans bound for export to make sure they couldn't germinate in foreign lands.

Despite the export precautions, seeds inevitably slipped out of Arabia. By 1616, Dutch traders had taken a plant from the Yemeni port of Mocha back home to Holland. At the time, Dutch merchants dominated global shipping, and they were responsible for spreading the plant to farther-flung places that included Ceylon—Sri Lanka, today—and Java, in modern-day Indonesia. They also planted coffee trees in an Amsterdam greenhouse. In 1714, the Dutch gifted one of these plants to King Louis XIV, who had it put into the *Jardin des Plantes* in Paris. The French propagated seedlings from it and eventually took them to Martinique, one of their Caribbean colonies. From there, the plants' descendants spread to Guatemala, El Salvador, Colombia, and, eventually, all over Latin America—including present-day Haiti. The Sun King's plant—the so-called "noble tree"—became the ancestor of billions of coffee trees throughout the Western Hemisphere. This narrow genetic stock is one reason that arabica coffee is susceptible to so many pests and diseases: 850 species of insects and 330 different fungi and bacteria attack the plant.[25]

All coffee grown in Haiti is arabica, and 90 percent of it is the typica variety—the same level of differentiation that people use to distinguish grapes in wines, like cabernet sauvignon, pinot grigio, or malbec.[26] Typica is an "heirloom," one of the oldest coffee varieties in production, relatively unchanged from the plants that were native to Ethiopia. Haiti's typica descended from the noble tree, almost certainly the same type of pyramidal plants that James Franklin described seeing during his 1820s visits. It has excellent potential for quality in terms of how it tastes in the cup, but it's a tall, spindly plant whose yields are just one-third of many newer varieties, like caturra or catuaí. So the height of Haiti's coffee trees is partly inevitable—it's wrapped up in the genetic makeup of the plant. Another reason for its low yields is that most older coffee varieties, typica included, are more susceptible to the hundreds of pests and diseases that plague coffee plants, especially a fungus called coffee leaf rust. The fungus' orangish spores cling to the underside of the plants' leaves, causing them to fall off, and can be spread for miles in the wind. A 2012 rust outbreak in Central America caused an estimated $1 billion in crop damage, decimating output in El Salvador, Costa Rica, and Guatemala.[27] It has wrecked the crop in Haiti in several recent years too, especially at lower-altitude farms, those below 1,000 meters in elevation.

Over the last century, agronomists have selected or bred many varieties of the coffee plant that have favorable traits, like resisting disease or being shorter, squatter, and higher-yielding. These newer varieties have caught on with farmers all over the coffee-growing world who are attracted to promises of better yields and incomes. Many of them, however, are arabica-robusta hybrids that taste inferior, a sticking point for quality-driven coffee roasters. While typica can produce an excellent cup, in the field it's the lowest-yielding of all the low-yielding varieties. That inefficiency presumably didn't bother colonial planters all that much, given that they used slave labor. But today, it's a challenge for small-scale farmers throughout Haiti's mountainous regions.

While new varieties have been developed over recent decades, global coffee production has also steadily grown. The three largest producer countries—Brazil, Vietnam, and Colombia—account for more than half the world's supply. Brazil, the top global producer, grows coffee like it's corn—monoculture, in full-sun, and with lots and lots of chemical fertilizers and pesticides applied on giant farms. Because it's a relatively developed country with high wages, Brazilians harvest the fruit mechanically, at least where the slopes are flat enough to drive combine-like machines down rows of coffee plants. The upshot is that the country has the most efficient farms and highest coffee yields in the world. Since it became a major coffee player two centuries ago, Brazil has made its name by growing huge quantities of not-necessarily-great-quality coffee.

By contrast, about 80 percent of the world's coffee is grown by an estimated 25 million smallholder farmers—a collectively large group of people who each grow a tiny amount of coffee on their tiny plots of land, often just a few acres in size. Haiti is a country of smallholders—85 percent of coffee farmers there have plots smaller than 5 acres. Much of coffee-growing East Africa, including countries like Ethiopia, Rwanda, and Burundi, practice small-scale farming as well. And while efficient farms on large tracts of land account for a huge chunk of coffee that comes from Latin America, you still find smallholder farmers all over Central and South America, often descendants of indigenous peoples who still live high in mountains like the Sierra Madre or the Andes.[28]

GLOBAL COFFEE PRODUCTION

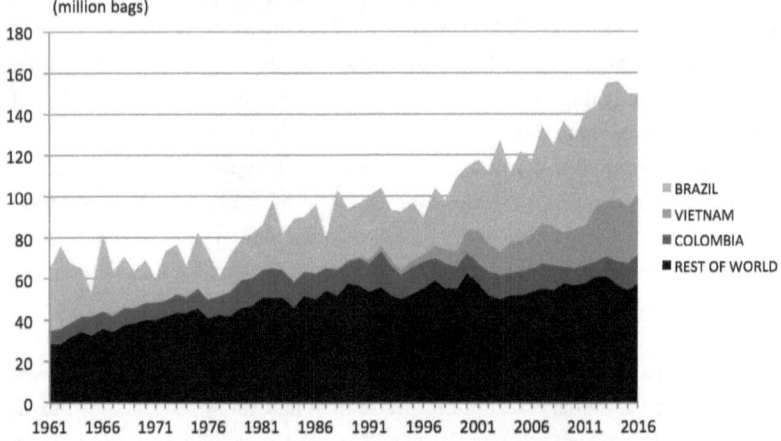

Global coffee production has been steadily rising for half a century. The three largest producers today are Brazil, Vietnam, and Colombia, who combine to produce more than half the world's coffee.[29]

The evolution of the coffee market presents those farmers with new opportunities, because the coffee people who have become obsessed with quality are willing to pay for it. "Today," George Howell says, in the coffee documentary, "we're starting to see cafes presenting coffees, and they're single farm, single origin, and they're not fair trade anymore only. They're now direct trade. This has now brought coffee farmers who are really caring, who are really craftsmen, it's allowing them for the first time to be independent of the commodity market and the swings that take place where for years in a row they could be paid under the cost of production."

That's the salient point if you're a small-scale coffee farmer in Haiti, or anywhere else for that matter. For most of the first half of 2016, the commodity market hovered between $1.15 and $1.35 per pound of green coffee. High-end coffee routinely sells for much higher than that—sometimes double or triple.[30] That entire price differential doesn't trickle down to the farm level for a small-scale grower to pocket. And because of the ways agriculture works and coffee is sorted for quality, farmers will never be able to produce excellent coffee with 100 percent of their crop—a portion won't meet specialty grade and will have to be sold into bulk markets. But if a grower can focus on high-end markets, then he or she can earn a hefty chunk of that price premium for quality.

The best opportunities for a farmer like Pierre Sanon, who has a small coffee plot with low yields and production, lie in this high-end segment. He'll never produce vast crops like those that come from Brazil. But he can focus on quality with the small crop that he does have, and, ideally, unhinge himself from the bulk market and make it easier to support his family.

These were the sorts of aims that Cantave and I had for the training program that we'd started with 350 farmer families in the region, and that was why we got up early to go visit the group in the mountains that November morning. It was also pretty much the exact same strategy that various aid agencies and NGOs had been trying to make work in Haiti since the 1980s, with little to show for it.

2

HOW HAITI BECAME HAITI

PRESIDENT WITH A PALACE

"IF YOU CAN talk while you work," Sonord Reby said, "and tell a joke every once in a while, then you'll work better." I told him I agreed. That afternoon he and a couple of the other employees who work on our demonstration farm were sweeping off a concrete patio, where coffee beans are dried once they've been harvested and separated from the fruity pulp of the cherry. I was joking with them about how our farm supervisor would always start to grumble if he thought the staff was chattering too much. Like most Haitians, Sonord, 26, comes from a large family. His dad died fairly suddenly from an illness a little before Christmas 2014, meaning that Sonord's job became even more important for the family, who he helps support.

Mistral Jean Louis, the supervisor, always has a story to tell, usually while laughing. He's a member of the family who owns the farm and partnered with the Haiti Coffee Academy to rehabilitate it. He claims to speak no English but I know him too well to believe it—he understands every word. He'd sometimes proclaim to visitors: "I'm a 100-percent Haitian original," before adding, "Not a photocopy!" His white beard and hair belie the fact that he's only in his 50s and strong as a bear.

Despite his genial nature, Mistral would have preferred complete silence from the farm employees. I preferred to let them rag each other about girls, or debate local politics or who was going to win the next Barcelona-Real Madrid soccer match. Sonord was born in 1990, the same year that Haiti held its first free presidential election—nearly two centuries after gaining its independence. Mistral grew up in what was a much different country than present-day Haiti—one where many people still thought that the only way to manage anything was with the iron fist of a dictator. A lot of Haitians, especially in rural areas, still feel the same way, talking of the supposed good ole days under the father-son Duvalier dictatorship. Papa Doc and Baby Doc, as they were known, held power for three decades, until 1986.

Well before that, the American novelist Zora Neale Hurston visited Haiti, as she described in her 1938 book, *Tell My Horse*. One passage has always stuck with me: "Of course Haiti is not now and never has been a democracy according to the American concept. It is an elected monarchy. The President of Haiti is really a king with a palace, with a reign limited to a term of years."[31] Except for the facts that the reign isn't always limited—see the Duvaliers—and the 2010 earthquake left the National Palace in a crumpled heap, most of her insights still seem spot on.

Cantave and I were usually on the same page when it came to management style, which made it easy to work together. That included letting the staff joke around while they worked. "This isn't a dictatorship anymore," Cantave said to me one day. He was seven when Baby Doc was ousted. "It hasn't been that way here for a long time."

Long before the days of the Duvaliers, Christopher Columbus shipwrecked on the northern coast of what later became Haiti. He called the island Hispaniola. Today, it's split into the Dominican Republic in the east and Haiti in the west.

Many Americans' familiarity with the place probably doesn't go much further than the understanding that a catastrophic earthquake hit there a few years ago, or beyond the international press's tagline for Haiti: "poorest country in the Western Hemisphere."

And there is definitely poverty in Haiti. The average economic output for a Haitian is $820 per year, way behind the neighboring D.R., whose citizens average over $6,000 a year. Over half of all Haitians are undernourished, compared to just 15 percent of Dominicans. Just one in four Haitians has access to a toilet. More than half of all adults cannot read. Money sent home by friends and family who live abroad powers almost a quarter of the economy. That's not too surprising once you know a figure that development economist Michael Clemens often cites: 80 percent of Haitians who have escaped poverty have done so not by staying in their own country but by leaving for the United States.[32] It's not far. I'd regularly fly home for holidays or a summer vacation. Sitting at the Miami airport on layovers, it always struck me that I was closer to Port-au-Prince than to my parents' home in Nashville.

A handful of Haitians have said the exact same line to me when it comes to visiting their country: Believe half of what you hear and nothing of what you see. On my first visit, in summer of 2010, I couldn't understand much of anything I heard. I spoke decent French after spending a year in Senegal in the Peace Corps, but people in Haiti don't really speak French, at least not the rank-and-file people. They speak Haitian Creole, a language largely based on French but one that someone fresh off a plane from Paris wouldn't understand. When it came to what I saw, it was exactly what most visitors notice when they first exit Toussaint Louverture International Airport—people, because they are everywhere in Port-au-Prince. Women clog all available sidewalk space selling fried plantains or second-hand clothes from the States. Young men weave in and out of makeshift traffic lanes on Chinese motorcycles. Anyone and everyone jumps into the street and wanders through the permanently gridlocked traffic barely bothering to look ahead, let alone both ways.

The best way I can describe the capital is by its friction—it feels like it's everywhere, and that you have to fight way more of it than should be necessary to get anything done. It manifests itself in the little things, like wasting an hour in line at the bank because the teller refuses to cash a check that was made out in blue ink but signed in black. Or the heavier things, like waiting six months for a power-tripping customs agent to decide to release a shipment of coffee seed from Brazil, despite having had approval from the Ministry of Agriculture all along.

After a few months, I bought a 200cc motorcycle to navigate the city, which eliminated a lot of the logistical friction. I could putter along in second gear between stand-still lanes of secondhand cars, water tankers, U.N. vehicles, and tap-taps—the brightly-painted mini-buses that shuttle ordinary Haitians to and fro and usually feature artwork of one, if not both, of the country's biggest superstars: Lionel Messi and Jesus. Still, even when you can avoid the traffic, you always feel like you're in a city of 3 million people built for maybe a tenth of that.

The entire country is only about the size of Massachusetts, but it's home to more than 10 million people. Steady formal employment is almost unheard of in rural areas, which is one reason that all five of our full-time farm employees had worked across the border in the D.R. at some point, either sharecropping for large landowners, or laboring on construction sites in Santo Domingo, or cutting sugar cane. About one out of every five Haitians has what we might consider a normal job—one that pays a steady wage. The other four split their time between unemployment and working in the informal sector, eking out a living that matches their circumstances: maybe driving a tap-tap in the city, or trading dry goods like spaghetti noodles in a border town, or growing coffee in the countryside. Today, these farmers' country literally does not appear on some lists of coffee-growing countries.[33] More than 200 years ago, however, the colony that predated Haiti was the world's biggest coffee producer.

AN UNTHINKABLE HISTORY

After Columbus' *Santa Maria* ran aground on Hispaniola on Christmas Day, 1492, the Spanish, French, and English spent the next two centuries fighting over the island. Pirates who sailed the Caribbean plundered merchant ships regardless of whose European flag the traders flew. Tortuga, a small island off the northern coast and part of present-day Haiti, became a haven for buccaneers. Meanwhile, the entire indigenous population—the Taíno people—quickly died out from the diseases the Europeans brought and the forced labor they subjected the natives to.[34]

In 1697, a treaty officially split the island between the French and Spanish. France called its colony Saint Domingue, and it promptly exploded in productivity through two crops: sugar in the lowlands and coffee in the mountains. By the late 1700s, Saint Domingue exported more sugar than Jamaica, Cuba, and Brazil combined. It also grew half the world's coffee. This colony the size of Massachusetts was more valuable than Britain's 13 American colonies combined. Saint Domingue had become the richest society on the planet. And all the riches were built on the backs of African slaves.[35]

Europeans had begun bringing slaves across the Atlantic and to the island in the 1500s—they needed new labor to replace the indigenous peoples dying off. The French worked them so brutally that half of all slaves died within a few years. It was cheaper to bring more from West Africa than to bother improving their living conditions in the Caribbean.[36]

Sugar cane, the colony's original cash cow, presented a few challenges: it required large and continuous tracts of land, had to be planted and harvested every six months, and needed massive amounts of slave labor to grow and costly mills and machinery to process. Because of the large investment required, sugar plantations were generally owned by the richest planters, most of whom were white Frenchmen. Coffee, on the other hand, was a simpler proposition. It takes up to four years for a coffee tree to give its first full harvest, but once a plantation is in production, it doesn't require nearly as much labor as sugar. I've heard from farmers in northern Haiti that the French first planted coffee in Dondon, a village that sits in a valley below La Citadelle, the largest fortress in the Americas. Other sources claim that coffee was first brought to Terrier-Rouge, another village in the North. Regardless of exactly where it was introduced, the crop eventually spread to every mountain region of Saint Domingue.[37]

The French colonists valued fertile flatlands more than land in the mountains, which was marginal for sugar and most other cash crops, including indigo and tobacco. But coffee didn't just require high altitude—it thrived at it. Plus, it could be profitable on small plots of land and with much less labor. The late Haitian academic Michel-Rolph Trouillot, of the University of Chicago, estimated that the average colonial coffee plantation used only about 20 slaves, while most sugar plantations required at least 100—along with six times as much initial investment in capital.[38] The need for relatively vast tracts of land to produce sugar was reflected in a 1789 count of plantations: there were just 288 of sugar to 2,009 of coffee.[39] Because of these dynamics, it was the *affranchis*, free men of color who were becoming increasingly influential both economically and politically, who owned many of Saint Domingue's coffee plantations. These *affranchis* were children of white French planters and female slaves; many of them inherited land from their fathers, and some were even sent to France to be educated.[40]

Haiti's tradition of small-scale farming has roots in this colonial era. Slaves not only worked the fields on their masters' sugar or coffee plantations, but they also kept their own gardens to supplement their diets, usually small plots of intercropped vegetables. That's not to say they were placated with the situation.

While Saint Domingue may have been incredibly productive, it was also a tinder box. Slaves eventually outnumbered free people 10 to 1—a census from 1789 put the count at nearly half a million slaves to roughly 50,000 free people. In late summer of 1791, a Jamaican-born slave led a midnight ceremony in the woods outside of the northern colonial capital, Cap-Français, now known as Cap-Haïtien. At the gathering, the slaves determined to revolt in a coordinated effort. By the following week, hundreds of sugar plantations across the colony's northern plain were afire. The ceremony became the catalyst for a bloody 13-year revolutionary war.[41]

The Haitian Revolution was far from black and white. Haiti's founding fathers had all fought for Napoleon under the French flag at various times. Political currents in Europe and the ebb and flow of the battlefield influenced who fought for and against whom during the course of the war—white planters, black slaves, French soldiers, mulatto freedmen. Eventually, the revolutionary generals and their troops battled the French at a place just below the Cap, driving them back into the harbor and onto a retreat to Europe. The slaves from Africa had defeated the world's most powerful empire of the time, creating just the second free republic in the Americas, after the United States. It remains the only country born of a successful slave revolution.

A few months before the final battle, one of the dark-skinned generals had symbolically cut the white center strip from the French *tricolore* flag to make a new one. At independence, in 1804, the military founders also gave the new country an old name—Haiti, the word for "land of mountains" in the native Taíno language. It was fitting given that nearly two-thirds of the country's land area has slopes of 20-percent grades or steeper.[42]

After independence, these military heroes were the obvious choices to lead the new country, similar to how George Washington was a natural pick for president after the American Revolution. Duke University historian Laurent Dubois has written that Haiti's new government "superficially resembled" that of the United States and other 19th-century democracies, but there was a key difference: "nearly all the political power was concentrated in one man's hands, without any meaningful opportunity for democratic opposition or protest."[43] This was the same king-with-a-term-limit way of governing that Zora Neale Hurston described more than a century after Haitian independence.

General Toussaint Louverture, the guy who now has an airport named after him, was the genius behind the revolution. He may have been born a slave but was destined to become the face of Haiti's independence. Just before the end of the war, French officials double-crossed him during supposed peace negotiations and banished him to Europe; he died alone in a dank prison in the Jura Mountains, a landscape that looked majestic the one time I saw it, on helicopter video coverage of a recent Tour de France.

Haiti's first constitution had declared Louverture Governor for Life. His right-hand general, Jean-Jacques Dessalines, succeeded him and went a step further upon coming to power: he proclaimed himself Emperor. The three rulers who immediately followed Dessalines, all former generals too, declared themselves either King or President for Life. Haiti's founders forged the country through warfare and then ingrained a precedent of near-absolute authority. It's proven hard to imagine the place being ruled any other way ever since.

FREE TO BE SUBJUGATED

During the revolution, sugar and coffee production plummeted, along with pretty much any economic activity not directly related to the war effort. After independence, the military elites who came to power looked for ways to help production recover. But the generals tried to rule the people as if they were still commanding armies. One of the first things Dessalines did was try to force the former slaves back onto the same plantations they used to work for lighter-skinned masters. This first generation of Haitians, who had just won their freedom with their blood, weren't thrilled about the back-to-the-fields strategy. So instead, they burned the remaining sugar mills and what little other infrastructure had survived the war. Many of them then fled to the mountains, where they claimed small plots that they could call their own, entrenching Haiti's culture of small-scale farming.

Early leaders also funded large standing armies and built forts and ramparts across the country to guard against another invasion, whether from the French or any other foreign power. They may have been overzealous fort builders—the Citadelle, for instance, has never once been used in battle—but their fears about foreign attacks weren't unfounded. At the time, other nations refused to recognize Haitian independence. A young United States with its own system of slavery wasn't going to grant legitimacy to a free black republic. And the French refused to accept the finality of their military defeat. The upshot was that no one wanted to trade with Haiti, at least not officially. And any stifling of commerce with the outside world certainly didn't help a fledgling nation striving to rebound its economic production.

In 1825, the French sent 14 warships to the harbor of the new capital, Port-au-Prince, threatening attack. Instead, in exchange for diplomatic recognition as free nation, Haiti's president agreed to pay France roughly $3 billion in today's terms. Haitians now sometimes say that they paid for their independence twice—first with their blood, and then with their money. They also sometimes say that coffee paid for that independence—coffee exports were taxed heavily to help make the debt payments, a tax that transferred wealth from poor farmers in the countryside to the central government in the capital. It took nearly 60 years to pay off the French indemnity.

The international trade did help Haiti's agricultural sector flourish for over a hundred years. The model was fairly straightforward: farmers produced food crops for local markets and coffee for export, along with some timber. The system spanned the country and was organized around provincial ports, as Haitian geographer Georges Anglade, who died in the 2010 earthquake, documented. "The spatial organization is regional, each of the 11 port cities home to powerful groups of landowners and traders active in importing and exporting," he wrote. "Coffee and logging transit systems converge in the regional cities. Towns and production areas are powered by their respective port."[44] Haitians farmed mostly on small-scale, family-owned plots, the structure still in place today. Many farmers still tend vegetable gardens and subsistence crops like manioc near the home, with plantings of cash crops like coffee farther away, often on a separate small holding. The diversified farming culture with roots in pre-independence Haiti even has a traditional name: *jadin Kreyòl*—Creole garden.[45]

By the 1820s, Haiti's coffee industry had rebounded to again become the top exporter in the world.[46] At the time, one-third of the coffee drunk in the United States came from Haiti. Coffee production thrived throughout much of the 19th century, providing livelihoods for people across the country, despite competition from slave-grown coffee in Brazil.[47] The fact that coffee could be profitable at small scale meant that free Haitians could be more prosperous growing coffee on their own small plots than by working on neighboring plantations that belonged to post-war elites. As Haiti was still the only independent nation in the Caribbean, it may well have been one of the best places in the Americas for people of African descent to live at the time.

While the country's production may have been rebounding, the debt deal with the French began to take its toll. By 1838, just 13 years after the agreement, Haiti's government spent 30 percent of its budget servicing the national debt. Almost 50 percent of funds went to the military. Less than 1 percent went toward education.[48] Victor Schoelcher, a French abolitionist who opposed the deal Haiti made with his country, visited around this time. Schoelcher was especially interested in the education system. He was bound to be disappointed. In Haiti he found "at most a thousand children who are taught to read and write in a population of 700,000 souls…"[49]

Around this time, the lasting effects of centralized power and a heavily funded military became clearer. From 1843 to 1915, Haiti had 22 heads of state; just one of them served his full term in office.[50] These decades of instability came down to coups and assassinations—plots to overtake government with force. And the plots invariably started within the army. To somewhat-paraphrase our American founding fathers: If you're going to have a large standing army, it's going to find work for itself.

Over those decades of instability, Haiti's population boomed, growing from 700,000 people in the 1840s to 2 million by 1910.[51] The population growth affected the agricultural sector because, as with sugar and coffee, there are two main requirements to grow any crop—land and labor.

American cafes and coffee roasters regularly stress how labor-intensive coffee production is. But coffee doesn't actually take all that much labor—at least not the growing of it—especially when compared to most crops farmers could be growing instead. One likely reason that people at the end of the supply chain fixate on the labor involved is that so many sets of hands touch the coffee before you take your first sip of it, from the grower all the way to the barista. But the historical comparisons from Saint Domingue speak to how much more labor a row crop like sugar requires. And while sugar may be particularly intensive, annual plants like beans and vegetables also require much more labor than coffee.[52] In the tropics, these row crops have two to three harvests per year, and each harvest means that farmers have to prepare fields, sow seed, apply fertilizers or organic material, and harvest crops. A perennial fruit tree like coffee, on the other hand, has just one harvest per year, and once trees have been planted and are in production they can produce for decades. Because coffee and other perennial cash crops require fewer hands, having suitable land available is often the crucial factor for growing them.

As Haiti's population grew throughout the 19th century, more and more offspring meant more and more hands available to work family farms—and also more mouths to feed. The swelling population also made land harder to come by because Haitians traditionally divide their farms into multiple plots to leave their children. So generation after generation, population grew, farm sizes shrunk, and population density ratcheted up. A handful of researchers, including Haitian agronomist Jean André Victor and Swedish economist Mats Lundahl, believe that these pressures became critical sometime in the late 1800s.

According to Victor, demand for food has been growing exponentially since about the mid-19th century. "To meet this growing demand," he writes, "more land has been cleared with a change in land use that promotes the expansion of row crops in the mountains and on slopes of more than 40 percent." Not only do row crops have shorter harvest cycles than coffee, they also bring the added benefit of putting food on the table to help feed extra mouths. The results of the land pressures, Victor writes, include erosion, fallowing of lands, and ever-worsening pests and diseases that attack wildlife and vegetation. "The agricultural system has become increasingly vulnerable to manmade shocks and natural disasters."[53]

Lundahl has noted that "there was enough land for everyone who wanted a plot at least up to the last quarter of the 19th century."[54] Fast forward to today, and the land is under way more pressure. Much of the country's forest cover has been destroyed to clear land for food crops, supply firewood and charcoal for cooking, or both. Soil fertility has been decreasing for half a century. And the population of that Massachusetts-sized area isn't just 2 million anymore—it's now over 10 million.[55]

While small-scale Haitian growers scratched out livelihoods in the face of population mathematics, the state did them few favors. As Michel-Rolph Trouillot put it, "The state was spending, but it was the peasant who was footing the bill."[56] The government raised virtually all tax revenue through customs duties and tariffs, including the export tax on coffee, which had replaced sugar as the key export after independence. Laurent Dubois writes that rural Haitians "carved out their own way of life in the countryside, but came to regard the state as a largely predatory force, at its best when it was absent altogether."[57]

But not all Haiti's ills were internal. Near the turn of the century, the increasingly influential United States proposed a deal with Haiti. Abraham Lincoln's administration had finally recognized Haitian independence during the Civil War, the U.S. the last world power to do so.[58] In the 1890s, President Benjamin Harrison, like other American heads of state before him, sought a deal to put a naval base at Môle Saint-Nicolas, on the northwestern tip of Hispaniola. In

1891, Anténor Firmin, the Haitian Minister of Foreign Affairs at the time, wrote the response to his counterpart, U.S. Consul General Frederick Douglass: No. Firmin and Haiti refused the deal on the grounds that the long-term lease proposed would cede too much sovereignty. The U.S. government wasn't happy but settled for a site across the Windward Passage, just 50 miles from the Môle as the crow flies: Guantanamo Bay, Cuba.

These tense dealings set the stage for more heavy-handed U.S. intervention. By the early 20th century, American banks held much of Haiti's debt, much of it by what is now Citibank.[59] In 1915, more than 150 political prisoners were executed by a Haitian military commander named Charles Oscar, whose tall frame and prominent teeth are forever in lore thanks to Haitians who still dress as him during Carnival. Oscar had carried out the murders at the behest of President Vilbrun Guillaume Sam, who was promptly dragged into the streets by a mob and literally ripped limb for limb. Williams Jennings Bryan, then the U.S. Secretary of State, had for years staunchly supported the idea of military intervention in Haiti. President Sam's murder in the streets presented a prime opportunity.[60] The U.S. government sent the Marines into Haiti in the summer of 1915. They stayed for two decades. The occupying force immediately took control of the treasury to make sure debts were repaid to American creditors. They also conscripted Haitian men across the countryside into what were basically chain gangs. Laborers who tried to escape were shot on the spot. When the Marines eventually pulled out, they'd left their mark on the country in the form of roads, some of which still stand today, that the conscripts were forced to build.

It was two decades later, in 1957, that François Duvalier won a rigged presidential election. The political innovation of the country doctor who came to be known as Papa Doc was something called the *Tonton Makout*—a secret police force and paramilitary network loyal to him above all else. It included a network of local magistrates, Vodou priests, and justices of the peace. The Makout are remembered in popular culture for the denim, red bandanas, and dark-tinted sunglasses they sometimes wore. They carried out thousands of political murders of opponents and served as Papa Doc's bulwark against army, that traditional source of coup and revolution. The force allowed Duvalier and his son, Jean Claude, to rule for three decades, until a popular uprising ousted Baby Doc in

1986.

The dictators taxed the people heavily, as the state had always done, both to finance the Tonton Makout and to funnel money into Swiss banks to create a vast fortune of their own. Papa Doc also handed out monopolies to his cronies, members of the small but opulent class of economic and political elites—a sugar industry here, a cement factory there. The state-sanctioned monopolies weren't subject to competition or the need to export, so it's not surprising that they weren't productive.[61]

There was also a heavy urban bias to the economy. Port-au-Prince was home to only 20 percent of the population, but the state doled out 80 percent of its expenditures there.[62] The government overwhelmingly pushed light manufacturing efforts—factories where Haitians assembled electronic harnesses, baseballs for MLB, or t-shirts and other textile products—that could put a lot of people to work quickly, albeit at low wages.[63] Haitians from the countryside flooded into the outskirts of Port-au-Prince and created slums that spawned entirely new problems. Haiti also quit producing nearly as much food as it had in the past. Agriculture had accounted for half of GDP in the 1950s but represented just a third by 1987.[64] And the trade from light manufacturing didn't come close to offsetting the decline. Haiti's trade deficit stood at $12 million in 1970; by 1980 it had risen to $183 million.[65]

Today, despite the fact that more than half of Haitians work in agriculture, the country imports 60 percent of the food it consumes. Much of it is subsidized American rice that may lower prices for Haitian households but serves largely as a boon to U.S. farmers—and makes it impossible for their Haitian counterparts to compete.[66] What good does it do to sell t-shirts to Americans if you have to squander all your earnings just to subsist on their imported food?

Despite the Duvaliers' brutal rule and human rights abuses, a lot of Haitians, especially in rural areas, remember the dictatorship years fondly. Standing beside a local guide one weekend at a trailhead in the mountains outside Jacmel, a southern coastal town known as the artistic capital of Haiti, I noticed a spray-painted wall that read, "VIVE J.C. DUVALIER." I asked the guide what was up with the Baby Doc graffiti. "It's because we respect Duvalier," he said. "The country was much better with him." That sentiment always made me think of the line about

Mussolini and his atrocities: "Yes, yes, but at least the trains ran on time!" If your dad wasn't disappeared by the Duvaliers, and if you remember the country having the security that comes along with a reign of terror, and better roads and schools than it's had recently, then you may feel nostalgia for the good ole days of iron fists. And sometimes, the sentiment may be born out of simple ignorance: over half of Haiti's population is under age 25.[67] The guide with me that day looked to be about my own age, in his late twenties. He wasn't even alive to remember what the Duvaliers' years in power were actually like.

It's hard to overstate just how damaging the Duvaliers were for Haiti, along with the political instability that followed the dictators. Not only did thousands of people disappear during their reign, but in 1960, Haiti and the neighboring Dominican Republic had the same GDP per capita; by 2005, Haiti's production per person was one-sixth of its neighbor—the D.R. had tripled while Haiti had halved.[68] At one point, Baby Doc appointed a Haitian former World Bank official as finance minister. The minister discovered that at least 36 percent of government revenues were being embezzled. He wasn't a minister for long.[69]

Despite the legacies of concentrated power, there are rich and long-standing traditions of local democracy in Haiti. For the most part, the country has had an elected parliament in place since 1816. And from the 1840s peaceful overthrow of an authoritarian president, to resistance throughout the countryside during the U.S. occupation, to the eruption of enthusiasm for elections after 1986, Haitians have been forming democratic grassroots movements for centuries. The problem is that the power brokers have ultimately prevailed every time, often claiming that the Haitian masses simply aren't ready for democracy.

Haiti was the only country in the world whose economy didn't grow during the 1950s and 1960s.[70] And during those mid-20th-century decades, the country finally reached a tipping point in the relationship between different types of crops.[71] For decades, the population growth that spawned a combination of scarce land and abundant farm hands had gradually been making labor-intensive food crops more attractive than land-intensive cash crops. When global coffee prices fell in the '50s and '60s, many rural Haitians abandoned the crop completely. Coffee, a long-term investment that's also subject to risky world markets, simply didn't work for small farmers any longer.

After coffee rebounded post-independence, Haiti had remained a top-10 coffee exporter for more than a century, until the 1950s. By the 1980s, it couldn't crack the top 25. Today, Haiti ranks 40th on the global list of coffee exporters.

HAITI HISTORICAL COFFEE EXPORTS
(thousand bags)

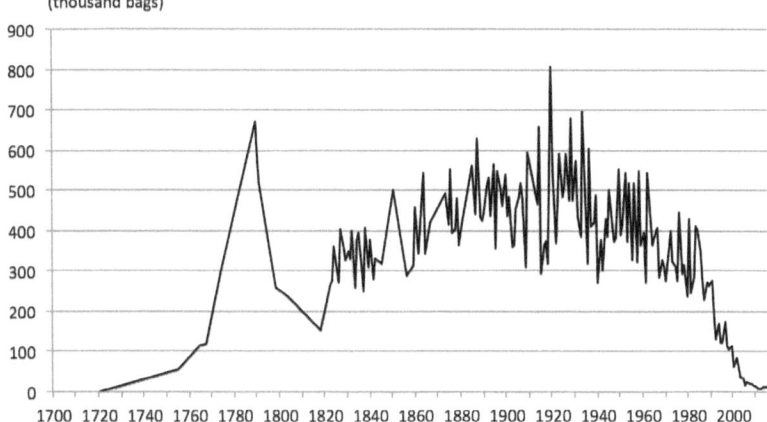

Haiti's export history from coffee's introduction to Saint Domingue in the early 1700s to present-day.[72]

Political scientist Simon Fass spent years in Haiti as a researcher and policy advisor in the '70s and '80s. "No government in the history of the territory from 1804 to 1986," Fass has written, "did anything of significance to improve the circumstances of ordinary people or to leave them with resources sufficient to permit productive investment and economic growth."[73] The state became essentially a private industry for personal gain. That was the reward, after all, that had motivated all those leaders to go through the trouble to knock off sitting presidents and seize power for themselves. It's not a stretch to say that the state as private industry was the fundamental institution that developed in Haiti.

James Franklin had touched on some of the same themes when writing about a fledgling Haiti all the way back in 1828. Some of them seem relevant even today, regardless of who happens to be sitting on the presidential throne at any given time: "From the present rulers it would be vain to expect any effort which might prove beneficial to the country...or to promote agriculture. The members composing the present government, seem to consider the poverty and ignorance of the people as the best safeguards of the security and permanence of their own property and power." Michel-Rolph Trouillot summarized the relationship between ordinary Haitians and their early post-revolution governments this way: "Peasants were the economic backbone of the nation; yet peasants had no claim whatsoever on the state." And Zora Neale Hurston, in another of her 1938 insights that still seems quite apt, described the state-as-private-industry this way: "In the past, as now, Haiti's curse has been her politicians. There are still too many men of influence in the country who believe that a national election is a mandate from the people to build themselves a big new house in Pétionville and Kenscoff and a trip to Paris."[74]

In light of the last 200-plus years, it's not surprising that Haiti today is a state more interested in short-term private gain than in building institutions that will help ordinary Haitians flourish.

3

THE COFFEE CHAIN

ALL ABOUT PROCESS

"NO, NO, YOU can't do it with water," Williams Prevot said. "It won't work." We were at a wet mill in Savane Zombie, the area in the mountains above town where Williams, who's in his early 40s, has lived and farmed his whole life. The wet mill, or washing station, is where farmers from the surrounding community bring their coffee to be transformed from a pulpy fruit into dried beans. Williams works at the mill and as a farmer trainer in our training program.

All About Coffee, a classic published in 1922, outlines 24 steps in the "evolution of a cup of coffee"—the steps it takes to get coffee from seed to cup.[75] I had asked Williams about the sixth step on the list, fermentation—specifically about whether the coffee beans sit in water during that part of the process or are left in the open air. Local custom and temperature play big roles in the specifics of the process. But the question was unfathomable for Williams, who had only ever done it open-air. In Haiti, there's often only one way to skin a cat.

TREE TO CUP

Unless you have a helicopter, there's no great way to get to southeastern Haiti. From Port-au-Prince, the drive to Thiotte takes about four hours, as long as you wake up early enough to get out of the city before daily gridlock sets in. You drive east out of the capital for about 45 minutes, passing flat sugar cane fields, signs advertising the E.U.-funded project re-doing the road, and, then, nothing but scrub acacia trees. A little before reaching the main border crossing with the Dominican Republic, you turn south and leave pavement. After going up a few small switchbacks, navigating a one-way section of road that clings to a cliffside, and driving through the middle of a dry river bed for half an hour, you start to climb. Villages are scattered along the entire route, as are villagers balancing loads of produce or water on their heads. Eventually, you top the ridge of the mountain chain, surrounded by decades-old pine trees and mist from clouds you've literally driven into, a landscape that always seemed as beautiful to me as it did incongruous with the Caribbean. This is the most aptly named national forest ever: La Forêt des Pins—the Pine Forest. Its footprint has shrunk by 80 percent since the beginning of the 20th century due to logging.[76] Today, in the heart of the forest, there's a weekly crossroads market that feels like a sea of people on Saturdays and a ghost town every other day, when hogs rummage through the mud and trash underneath vendors' vacant stick-pole stands. Leaving the forest, you drop down the southern side of the mountain range, passing the coffee washing station near Williams' house, at about 1,400 meters altitude. After more switchbacks than I ever cared to count, the town of Thiotte and its four paved blocks open up in front of you, about 900 meters above the sea, which you can see stretching into the distance.

The only thing worse than doing that drive in the rainy season was doing it during the dry one, when our gray 4x4 pickup truck would be covered with a coat of white dust by the time we arrived. For those of us who live far from the equator, it's easy to overlook the fact that coffee is an agricultural product that depends on harvest cycles and weather patterns.[77]

In southeastern Haiti, it hardly rains from Christmas to Easter. Every spring the rains finally arrive and break the months-long dry season. Shortly afterward, white blossoms that look like miniature starfish start to appear on coffee trees. The flowers drop after just a few days, and clusters of tiny green fruits begin to develop on the branches in their place. After seven or eight more months the green fruits turn to yellow as they start to ripen. Then, in late August or September, the cherries on lower-altitude trees near town begin to turn red. The harvest starts later and lasts longer as you climb higher and higher—the cooler temperatures at higher altitudes slow down the development of the fruit, which also adds complexity and flavor to the coffee.

The coffee cherry itself is like an onion—it's layered. Underneath the outer skin is a fruity pulp, then another covering called parchment, and finally a thin layer called silver skin, which surrounds the seed, or bean, itself. Each cherry that develops properly contains two oblong seeds.[78]

Once the cherry has developed on the tree, there's nothing that anyone along the supply chain can do to increase the potential quality inherent to the beans inside. But about a million things can be done to keep that coffee from reaching its potential. And it all starts at harvest.

Because spring rains are sporadic, coffee flowering is too. The uneven rains show through months later in the uneven ripening of coffee cherry. In late fall, a single plant might be loaded with a mixture of green, yellow, and red cherries.[79] This throws a wrench into harvesting, because the one thing that improves coffee quality most is harvesting only ripe cherry. In much the same way that a green banana tastes harsh and unpleasant, under-ripe cherries give coffee an astringent or grassy taste. Over-ripe cherries start to blacken and dry while still on the branch, leading to over-fermented or yeasty flavors that can ruin a batch of coffee entirely. But the sugars inside fully ripe, deep-red cherries are fully developed and will yield the best cup possible.[80]

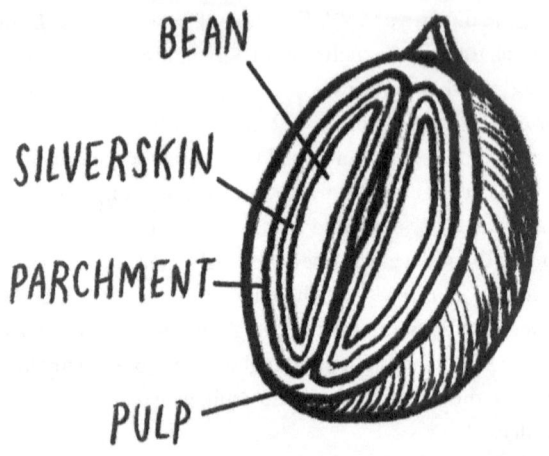

COFFEE CHERRY
(CROSS-SECTION)

Where labor is cheap farmers pick coffee by hand so that they can selectively harvest it. That includes smallholder countries like Haiti, where family members, often women and children, usually handle the picking. It also includes countries where the owners of large farms and estates hire pickers, often transient workers, to harvest by hand. In smallholder countries farmers don't generally count the labor as a cost, at least not in a traditional accounting sense. But it's a considerable time cost at the least—over the several months of a season, pickers have to make multiple passes over the same trees if they want to get only ripe cherry.

The minimum wage in Haiti is about $100 per month. In Brazil, it's about triple that, which is one reason it's economical for many farms there to harvest coffee with machines—robot wages are notoriously cheap. Tractors drag mechanical harvesters over the top of coffee rows, engulfing the shrubs while fiberglass rods agitate the branches to knock cherries into a receptacle. Farmers try to time harvest to the peak ripening period, but some variation is unavoidable. "The shock for a traveling coffee buyer on their first trip to Brazil," says Thompson Owen, founder of Oakland-based coffee importer Sweet Maria's, "would be to see coffee fruit, from raw green, to semi-ripe to over-ripe and dried pods, all picked and piled up at once."[81] Coffee cherry is generally sorted after harvest anyway, but the sorting of mechanically harvested coffee has to be much more intensive than for a selectively picked one.

In Haiti, coffee can take a few different paths after harvest. Today about 95 percent of it never leaves the island of Hispaniola. The majority of it supplies the Haitian market, but up to a third of all production is sent across the border informally to buyers in the Dominican Republic, often by mule or on foot. Maybe 5 percent of total production is headed abroad as official exports.[82] And where a coffee is bound influences what's done to the cherry after harvest—what's known as the processing method.

The ultimate goal of processing coffee is to dry the seed, or bean, so that it can be kept without spoiling, shipped to a buyer, and eventually roasted. You can choose to dry the coffee bean in one of three basic forms: with the whole cherry still around it; with the fruit mechanically separated from the bean, a sugary layer still clinging to it; or with both the fruit separated and the sugars removed, leaving the parchment layer as the outer covering.

The traditional way to process cherries, whether in coffee's homeland in Ethiopia, or in the first places it was cultivated on the Arabian Peninsula, or in the Caribbean, is to leave them in the sun to dry and shrivel up like raisins. Today, there are many variations on how this is done. In Ethiopia, for example, some cooperatives pick and sort ripe red cherry and dry it on raised tables that allow for maximum airflow. These can yield highly prized and highly priced coffees with interesting fruity flavors—some of them taste like getting smacked in the face with a handful of blueberries. But there's often much less quality control involved. In Haiti, farmers fortunate enough to have concrete patios at their mountain homes dry cherries there. I've also seen farmers use empty rice sacks, banana leaves, or their dirt yards. Every fall in Thiotte, one resident in town spreads his coffee on the same small section of paved street in front of his house, evidently not bothered by the teenagers who run over it with their motos.

After a few weeks of sun-drying coffee cherries, you wind up with shrunken and blackened fruit. The dry black crust then has to be hulled off the coffee beans contained inside. The hulling can be done with a machine or by hand with a mortar and pestle. This traditional method is called the dry process, and the resulting coffee is referred to as "natural" or "unwashed" coffee.[83] These coffees are full-bodied in the cup and can have those intense, fruity flavors. But most of the dry-processed coffee produced around the world is low quality. The method can be done on the farm or in the home with simple technology, at low cost, and with lax quality control, the resulting coffee destined for bulk markets that prioritize volume.

According to Haiti's National Coffee Institute, about two-thirds of the country's coffee is dry-processed. Most of it is too low quality to pass muster for export. Back in the sector's heyday, Haitian coffee exporters bought in bulk from the rural regions where their families had roots, transported the coffee to Port-au-Prince, and sorted it into various grades, reserving the best for international buyers. So even though they bought in bulk, which included a lot of bad coffee, they could sort out the best beans for export, and sell the rest on the local market.

Nearly all those exporters have left the coffee business. Growers now sell to whoever shows up at their door first with cash in hand, whether that buyer is a female merchant who trades in agricultural produce of all types, an agent from one of the handful of remaining exporters and industrial roasters in the capital, or a Dominican.[84] And because small-scale growers are invariably cash-strapped—often already in debt to friends, family, or neighbors—many can't afford to wait for coffee to ripen fully or be all that concerned with quality. A little cash in hand today is worth much more to them than the potential payoff that comes months later by picking and processing only ripe, quality cherries.

Today, the vast majority of the coffee sold by roasters and cafes in the United States, from the ubiquitous Starbucks to high-end shops like Stumptown and Blue Bottle, is processed in a different way—the wet process, which yields what's called "washed coffee." Wet-processed coffees are generally clean and consistent in the cup, and many have an interesting brightness to them, what coffee cuppers refer to as acidity. The method, however, is more intensive and costly than dry processing and requires specialized equipment and infrastructure. In one spot in southeastern Haiti, it happens at the mill where Williams works during coffee harvest.[85]

In 1991, about 150 farmers in the area officially organized, calling themselves the *Association des Paysans Agricoles de Savane-Zombie*. Each farmer owns a small plot of land, so each can produce only a small amount of coffee. And these farmers all know each other—they grew up together, farm together, go to church together. By organizing into the association, which essentially operates as a cooperative, they can collect a large enough quantity to attract a foreign buyer and to justify the costs of processing a shipment for export.

Williams is technically the organization's secretary, but he acts as the lead processor as well, overseeing the handful of other mill workers and controlling for quality along the way. When harvest begins, farmers bring their coffee cherry to the wet mill, the afternoon of the day it's been picked. The association pays the farmers a set price at delivery, in cash, with the expectation that a second payment —called the *ristourne*, or rebate—will be paid once the coffee has landed at a buyer's warehouse abroad and funds have been remunerated back to the association. This is a huge hurdle to coffee groups in Haiti and everywhere. They're competing against many other local buyers, and without financing that allows them to pay cash, no farmer would bring them coffee—the promise of payment in six months won't feed a farmer's family or pay his kids' school fees. Organizations like Cambridge-based Root Capital, which works in Haiti, have made tackling this issue their mission, but it's a mammoth proposition. Financing a coffee cooperative in rural Haiti isn't a calling for the risk averse.

When the cherries arrive at the mill, Williams dumps them into a concrete basin of water. The ones that float—the less-dense, underdeveloped ones—are skimmed off to be sold on the less-discerning local market. The good cherries are then fed into a depulper, a machine that has a stationary disc and rotating drum that separate the fruity pulp from the seeds inside. It's vital to pulp the cherries no more than about 12 hours after they're picked, or else they can start to ferment and go bad. The pulper Williams operates is old-school, and inefficient—it's hand-cranked. This works in Haiti, where production is quite low, but the modern way is to use a belt connected to a motor that turns the depulper. The red pulp exits one side, to be composted and later used as fertilizer. The seeds exit the other side into another concrete basin, where they're left to ferment until morning, a process that's closely monitored. This is the step I had asked Williams about when he looked at me incredulously—fermentation duration varies depending on local temperature, as does the decision of whether to submerge the beans in water during this step.

The fermentation breaks down the moist and sugary layer of pulp, called mucilage, which still clings to the seeds after the pulp has been removed. Williams knows when the fermentation is finished from the gritty feel of the beans and the squeaking sound they make when he rubs them between his hands. He then transfers the coffee into a series of basins where the beans are washed in multiple rounds of clean water, which rinses away the broken-down mucilage. After washing, the beans are spread across a concrete patio with a wooden coffee rake. They dry in the sun for about seven to 10 days, and once dry, the beans are covered by the parchment layer, a tan-colored papery husk. This entire process happens regularly with many batches as farmers bring cherry to the wet mill over the course of months, from about late November to early February in Savane Zombie.

In early 2015, parchment coffee bound for La Colombe sat at the Savane Zombie wet mill. Williams, Cantave, and I checked it regularly with a handheld battery-powered device that measures the moisture content of the beans. Once all the coffee had reached the ideal moisture level, between 10 and 12 percent, we bagged it and sent it to Port-au-Prince. The truck took it to the dry mill at Geo Wiener, a fourth-generation Haitian coffee exporter. At the dry mill, basically a small factory, a huller milled off the parchment and spat out what's known as green coffee—raw, dried, and unroasted coffee beans.

The coffee still had to be sorted. Green coffee beans aren't uniform in size or color, and broken, insect-damaged, and underdeveloped beans inevitably slip through during processing. After hulling, a series of screens with different-sized holes sort the beans by size. Some mills then feed the coffee onto slickly engineered Brazilian-made tables that vibrate incessantly; the movement and slant of the tabletop sorts out bad beans based on density. But most of this sorting is still done by hand in Haiti, usually by women. Once finally prepped, workers packaged the Savane Zombie coffee into jute bags, which they had first lined with polyurethane bags that extend the shelf life of the raw beans. Each bag holds 60 kilograms of green coffee, about 132 pounds, which is the standard size in Haiti and many other countries. The bags were loaded into a shipping container, which was sent down the street to the port and onto an ocean liner. After a few days at sea, some customs red tape, and a truck shipment, La Colombe received it in Philadelphia in late spring. There, they roasted the coffee, transforming it into the brown beans that most consumers are more familiar with, and sold it as "Savan Zombi," the Creole spelling of the coffee's place of origin.

A HANDSOME ROAST

While home during one break from Haiti I visited Crema, a small husband-and-wife-owned roastery in Nashville that's won multiple national awards, to take part in a coffee cupping with roaster and green coffee buyer Winston Harrison. In the small room that houses the 12-kilogram Diedrich coffee roaster in the back of the cafe, he set up a series of small ceramic bowls, filled each one with coffee grounds from a different country, and steeped them in water slightly below boiling. We first smelled the aromas coming off the coffees, before tasting them with soup spoons as they cooled.

"We always look for coffee that scores an 85 and above," Harrison had written me in response to an email about what he looks for when buying coffee. The 85 he mentioned refers to cup score. Technically, a specialty coffee is one that scores 80 or above on the 100-point scale that professionals use to evaluate coffees when cupping.[86] Roasters receive air-shipped samples as soon as they're available during early harvest, and the samples inform buying decisions and price negotiations. A score from a single cupping isn't necessarily the be-all end-all for that coffee. Taste is, after all, subjective, and two different buyers evaluating the same 10 coffees may make very different decisions about which ones to purchase. But cup score is an integral tool when it comes to comparing coffees. "If we don't taste the quality," Harrison continued, "we will not buy it."

Whether from your local roaster or Starbucks, most specialty coffee is washed, partly because these wet-processed coffees taste clean, crisp, and slightly sweet in the cup—they're what the market wants. La Colombe described the Savan Zombi coffee as having hints of lavender, orange, and caramel. William Ukers, the 1922 author of *All About Coffee*, described Haitian washed coffee generally, noting that it "has a rich, fairly acid, mildly-sweet flavor…"[87]

When it comes to dry processing, the main issue is consistency. It's possible to wind up with a great quality coffee, but because you dry the coffee with fruit still around the bean, there's more moisture and volatility involved. It's easy for the coffee to get moldy or over-fermented. With the wet process, there are many variables that can alter end quality, but you more or less know what you're getting. So as a general rule, if you dry process coffee, quality is not the ultimate goal.

Haiti is no exception. The focus on quantity over quality made sense in the past —when the country actually had quantity as a significant global coffee producer. "Sometimes the crop is gathered hastily," Spenser St. John, a British *chargé d'affaires* to Haiti, wrote in 1889. "Ripe and unripe seeds are mixed; and then it is dried on the bare ground, regardless of the state of the weather; and when swept up into heaps it is too often intermingled with small stones, leaves, and dirt; and fraudulent cultivators or middle-men add other substances to increase the weight." His description from more than 100 years ago sounds little different from the practices I've seen in Haiti, from the lack of care in dry processing to the adding of twigs, rocks, or milled corn to stretch quantity. Ukers reported much the same: "the trees were largely permitted to fall into a wild natural state, and little attention was given to them or to the handling of the crop."[88]

Ukers and other historical accounts note that while both wet and dry methods have been used to a degree, most Haitian coffees have always been dry-processed. "When properly grown and cured," he wrote, "they rank well with high-grade washed varieties, and have a rich, fairly acid flavor in the cup. The bean is blue-green, and makes a handsome roast." The focus on dry process makes sense in context of the historical export market: Europe. Natural coffees tend to be full-bodied and favored for espresso blends, so Haitian coffees were perfectly suited to satisfy European tastes. Ukers notes that Haitian coffee was "a great favorite" of the French. The other traditional export markets were Belgium, Italy, and, to an extent, American markets like New Orleans.[89]

Today, virtually all Haiti's official coffee exports—still only about 5 percent of total production—are wet-processed. Which isn't to say that the rest is dry processed—a good chunk falls somewhere in between. So-called "pulped-natural" coffees—known as *tchoka*, in Haiti—are increasingly popular in the industry. To prepare it, the cherries are pulped as in the wet method, but rather than washing the beans, drying is begun immediately, with the sugary mucilage still intact. That sticky layer helped coin another term for the method: honey process. The taste of these coffees, unsurprisingly, lies somewhere between those of wet- and dry-processed ones—pulped naturals are usually fuller-bodied and less acidic than washed coffees, but have less intense flavors than unwashed ones. In Haiti, countless farmers follow some variation of this method, especially in border areas. Some of them have small, often ancient, hand-crank depulpers, but many use wooden mortars and pestles to separate the beans from the pulp. Much of this pulped-natural coffee goes to the D.R.—it's much less bulky to send pulped coffee beans across a mountain on a donkey than to send whole cherry.[90]

While washed coffee dominates the U.S. specialty market, with care and attention, it's possible to produce an excellent quality coffee following any of these processing methods. Factors like altitude and farm maintenance contribute to the quality ceiling for any given coffee. But if you take great care after harvest—sort and use only ripe cherry, for instance, or pay attention that coffee doesn't over-ferment and ruin—then either wet, dry, or honey processing can yield a high-quality coffee.

These days, the bar for many quality-driven roasters is that cup score of 85 or higher. And if there's one trait that roasters favor beyond quality, it's uniqueness. A coffee with an interesting or surprising taste or origin stands out, whether on the cupping table or the menu, and companies want to have a coffee on their pour-over or espresso bar that no other roaster has. This is one reason that some naturals and honey-processed coffees have taken off in recent years. It's also a reason that a lot of roasters obsess over tales about coffee sourcing and origins.

Because coffee harvests are staggered throughout the year across Latin America, Africa, and the Pacific, roasters can constantly offer new and fresh beans year-round. People debate exactly how long green coffee will maintain quality while being stored in a roastery or warehouse, but the standard is to get rid of all coffee from a current year before the new crop comes in—a quality-driven roaster never wants to be selling last year's crop. Freshness is most important for single-origin coffees, like the Savan Zombi one. These have to stand on their own in the cup, as opposed to a blend, which might be made with a handful of coffees of differing quality from around the world.

La Colombe sold out of the Savan Zombi coffee after just a few months. It had obviously cleared the first requirement to be exported—the quality bar. But you can find good specialty coffee in at least 20 countries. One reason it sold like hotcakes was its uniqueness—as the export figures show, you can hardly find Haitian coffee in the U.S. today, whether washed or not.

THE HAITIAN COFFEE FARMER

The first time I rode my motorcycle across Port-au-Prince to visit the National Coffee Institute, INCAH, the first thing that caught my eye was a row of green John Deere tractors lined up in front of the Ministry of Agriculture building. They looked new. I took a photo with my iPhone and wondered who paid for them.

Jobert Angrand, INCAH's head, asked if I wanted coffee. It arrived in small terra cotta cups on a tray. Haiti takes its lead from France when it comes to coffee drinking—and French coffee is dark, strong, and "sucks so bad," as food and coffee writer Oliver Strand has put it. But, Strand added, "the point of a Parisian cafe isn't really the coffee."[91] To me, the point of drinking coffee in Haiti always seemed to be the sugar. The traditional Haitian coffee roast is what I can only describe as dark-to-burnt. It's practical. Except for at a few cafes and restaurants in the capital, the quality of the coffee is usually sub-par, so you have to roast it really well-done to cover the defects. And once it's roasted that dark, you need half a cup of sugar just to get it down. A lot of Haitians still roast coffee at home, in a pot over a charcoal fire, and most mix sugar into the beans as they roast. It comes out looking like a gooey, sparkling black mass, before being ground with a mortar and pestle. There's an old joke that Haiti is 80 percent Catholic and 100 percent Vodou. It's probably also close to 100 percent coffee drinker. Many families, whether in the city or country, drink coffee every morning, often with a piece of bread or avocado to help fill an empty stomach at the start of the day.

Angrand lamented that despite various aid efforts, too little investment in the coffee sector has gone toward production, given its declines. One reason coffee is popular with aid groups is that it has environmental benefits in addition to economic ones. Much of Haiti is severely deforested, but because coffee trees need shade, Angrand explained, half of the country's remaining forested areas have coffee. "It can protect the land," he said, "and it's an important market."[92] The agency operates nurseries in Haiti's four major coffee areas to help farmers replant.[93] But its work is limited, as is the research done at INCAH's lab, which is "not serious," Angrand, who studied agronomy in Port-au-Prince and agroforestry in Costa Rica, admitted. "We have to keep up with our research or else we'll lose our coffee industry." He told me that a coffee plant's best-producing window is from years five to 15, adding that in Haiti, most trees are over 20 years old. He compared that to Colombia, where an INCAH delegation visited in recent years, saying that most trees there are less than nine years old. It's common practice in much of Latin America to stump trees—chop them off completely with a machete about a foot from the ground—every five to eight years. During a weeklong trip to Guatemala last summer, Cantave and I didn't visit a single farm that didn't do this. Stumped trees go out of production for a year or two, so farmers follow a farm-wide rotation, but the new trunks will redevelop into rejuvenated, high-yielding plants. But most smallholders, whether in Haiti or East Africa or elsewhere, can't justify the trade-off of lost immediate production in return for longer-term gains. And virtually every Haitian coffee farmer is a smallholder.

In reality, you'd be hard pressed to find a single Haitian who describes themselves as a "coffee farmer." In their own words they'd most likely be just a "farmer," largely due to the diversified Creole-garden style of farming that's been practiced for so long. Coffee plots are particularly diverse—the plants typically grow among orange, local grapefruit, banana, and other fruit trees, as well as taller shade trees like tropical laurels and oaks. When it comes to food crops, beans and corn are probably the two most popular and are cultivated all across the country. In the southeastern mountains, farmers also grow a lot of potatoes, tropical cabbage, and carrots, some of which help feed the family and some of which can be sent to regional markets to bring in income. On the southern peninsula, which juts out to the west, you find yams growing all over the mountainous coffee areas.[94] Haitian farmers intercrop anything with everything. If you have a small plot of land, it only makes sense to diversify. You minimize risk by not placing all your eggs in one basket.

Among the many options, growing coffee can—in theory—be most profitable because it can be successful at a very small scale. But that's only if farmers can overcome the various challenges that come with cultivating it. Coffee's long-term outlook compared to row crops makes the investment of time and energy difficult. In Haiti, modern coffee yields have become so pitiful that beans and corn wind up being more profitable for many farmers. Global coffee markets and prices are also notoriously volatile. Weather patterns, like the three-year drought that crippled agricultural production in parts of Haiti recently, can be fickle and devastating. Diseases like leaf rust can destroy a grower's coffee farm in a single season. And if the fungus doesn't get your crop, coffee borer beetles might—the insects bore into cherries as they develop and have damaged up to half of the coffee harvest in certain Haitian communities in recent seasons.

A more fundamental source of impediment, however, is the political foundation that the country is built on. It's probably not a stretch to say that Haiti has been saddled with political instability since 1986—and it may be just as accurate to peg the year at 1804, if not 1492. But take just 1986, the year the people finally uprooted the Duvaliers. That year represents the start of what Haiti-born University of Virginia political scientist Robert Fatton has called "the unending transition to democracy." The ouster of the dictators and promise of democracy brought a wave of optimism to Haitians and outside observers alike. But, Fatton says, many of those people missed a crucial factor. To transition to democracy, Haiti would have to replace not only a regime—the father-son duo who just happened to be the latest rulers to warm the throne. It would also have to replace an entire form of government—the historical institution of dictatorship that had roots two-centuries deep.

"In a country where destitution is the norm and private avenues to wealth are rare," Fatton has written, "politics becomes an entrepreneurial vocation, virtually the sole means of material and social advancement for those not born into wealth and privilege. Controlling the state becomes a zero-sum game, a fight to the death to monopolize the sinecures of political power."[95]

In the 30 years since 1986, there have been 18 separate terms served by heads of state. That includes interim and acting presidents, like the one in power today as a result of years of political impasse and delayed elections. In theory, and in a world without coups, there should have been just six terms over those three decades, given that the term limit for a Haitian president is five years. I'm not qualified to say whether Haiti today lies closer to dictatorship or democracy, but few people would try to argue that the transition is complete.

Because that transition has been never-ending, an entire generation has now passed since 1986 full of political uncertainty about the future. And the political bleeds into everything—the international embargo of the early 1990s that crippled the economy, the riots and insecurity of the mid 2000s that wracked the country, and the response to the 2010 earthquake, with its wave of foreign aid that swamped everything in its path for better and worse.

The uncertainty also undergirds the day-to-day choices made by all Haitians, rural farmers included. It's not by accident that most coffee plantings in the country lie somewhere between neglect and all-out abandonment. If you're unsure what the political winds will bring next year, or who might be in power and how it will affect you, then why invest in a long-term cash crop that takes years for a payoff? You'd be wiser to focus on the food-crop harvest that's a few months away and make sure you provide for your family, which is exactly what Haitian farmers do.

While coffee production has been steadily increasing for decades worldwide, it's been dwindling in Haiti, and official exports have nearly bottomed out. Thirty years ago, there were more than 20 coffee exporters in the country. Today, there are just two main companies left, plus a handful of minor ones that are only active in years when the harvest is up. Haiti now produces approximately 300,000 bags of coffee each year, about 0.2 percent of global production.

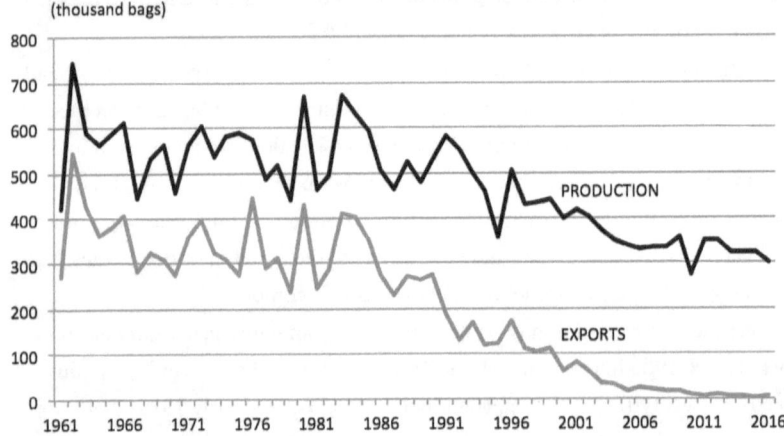

HAITI COFFEE PRODUCTION AND EXPORTS
(thousand bags)

While global coffee production has steadily risen for 50 years, Haitian production and exports have notably declined.[96]

The decline has not been for lack of desire to turn the sector around, at least not from outsiders with aid money to spend. While researching Haiti's sector, I estimated that at least $25 million in aid had been spent exclusively on coffee projects over the past 25 years. So, despite all that spending, if you look at any data point on Haiti's coffee industry, or talk to any coffee grower in the country for that matter, why does the picture still look so bad?

4

MISADVENTURES IN AID

A WEAK STATE

BILL CLINTON HAD a helicopter when he came to Thiotte. One afternoon in early 2014, the day before Clinton arrived, I watched the helicopter land on a concrete patio a stone's throw from town at the estate of one of the oldest families in the area—pretty much the only home in the area that would qualify as an "estate." An advance team of agents who detail former presidents on trips like this one had already done a security check the day prior, and the pilot was now doing his test run. His attempted landing at a nearby soccer field had apparently kicked up too much dust, and the concrete patio was the largest surface around, for drying coffee or landing a helicopter. The next day, it landed again, this time with Clinton inside. A few minutes later, he and a convoy of black-windowed diplomatic corps SUVs arrived at our coffee farm and nursery.

Clinton visits Haiti regularly. His relationship with the country goes back decades, both personally and politically. By January 12, 2010, the day of the earthquake, he was the U.N. Special Envoy to Haiti. I'd seen him once in Port-au-Prince at a small press conference about business investment in the country. He often visits the projects and businesses that his family foundation backs. At the demonstration farm that day, he seemed to enjoy seeing the nursery full of seedlings and hearing Cantave explain the intricacies of growing coffee, as an American colleague of ours translated the French for Clinton. Afterward, the former President lingered to pose for pictures with some of the Haitian workers and the other American visitors.

Clinton may have been the most recognizable foreign dignitary involved in the post-disaster reconstruction efforts, but he was hardly on his own. Between foreign governments and international organizations like the United Nations, $10 billion was pledged to help Haiti rebuild after the 2010 earthquake. In each of the two years that followed, an average of $3 billion was disbursed. For frame of reference, the size of Haiti's entire annual economy at the time of the quake was $6 billion. It was impossible for that much money to come into the country that quickly without having huge effects, both positive and negative.[97]

To be fair, not all that money was actually spent in Haiti. To take one example: tons of U.S. bottled water were flown into Port-au-Prince to be distributed to survivors for months after the disaster. But there were still a handful of working water plants in Haiti. Maybe flying water in for a few weeks made sense. But if any city already had an antiquated network to distribute drinking water on foot—exactly the type that could function in the aftermath of an earthquake—it was Port-au-Prince. You can't throw a 5-cent *gourde* piece on the capital streets without hitting a kid carrying a sack full of packets of treated water on his head, and those 5 *gourdes* would buy you two or three of them. But the local companies that produce those water packets were displaced by the free water coming in. Buying local could have not only saved on the costly air-freight for all those pallets of bottled water, but it also could have pumped money into a teetering economy, paying water makers and ordinary Haitians who could have made deliveries to survivors in tent camps and throughout the city.[98]

Top-down, outsider-driven action was the default after the disaster.[99] One investigation found that of the nearly $400 million that USAID, the aid arm of the American government, awarded in the two years following the earthquake, less than 1 percent went to Haitian firms and organizations. Most of that U.S. government funding barely left the shadow of the Washington Monument—77 percent went to aid contractors in the D.C. area.[100] Those contractors all have their own office rents and expat salaries and business-class airfares to pay before the money trickles down to the people it's ostensibly helping. When it came to trying to coordinate these numerous agencies and NGOs involved in the response, the groups held meetings at the main U.N. base in the capital. The meetings sometimes took place in French, sometimes in English, and never in Haitian Creole. And in addition to MINUSTAH, the peacekeeping force that had been in the country since 2004, more than 20 different U.N. agencies were operating in Haiti after the quake, one of them just to work out the logistics for all the rest.[101]

Because so much of the recovery was led by foreigners, like those U.N. agencies or aid workers from abroad, it was easy to forget the group of people who outsiders so often love to lump together when writing about the place—the people of Haiti. If you were an official in D.C. with little prior knowledge of Haiti and its history, culture, and local context, then it may never have crossed your mind that the place would still have functioning water plants post-quake. But many people far away in Washington and Geneva were making decisions about how billions of dollars would be spent. It seems like an especially weird thing to happen to Haiti, an unabashedly proud country that refused to abide that U.S. naval base a century ago, and that once had a constitution making it illegal for foreigners to own land or whites to become citizens.[102]

Ultimately, the funding boost that followed the earthquake was just the latest deluge in a legacy of decades of aid saturation. In recent years, outside aid to Haiti's government has swamped the national budget—the year before the quake, for instance, total aid was 1.3 times larger than government revenues.[103] The bulk of the tax revenue the government can muster internally comes from either customs fees or a tax on consumption, a regressive policy that punishes poor people, who wind up handing over a much higher portion of their earnings than the rich.[104] And for over two centuries, Haiti's governments have never seemed too concerned with using their revenue or authority to build institutions that would help the people thrive. When you examine Haiti today, you'd almost expect to find a state more interested in short-term gain than creating and maintaining a functioning education sector, good roads, a reliable power grid, or a fair judicial system.

When external aid becomes more important than internal revenue, who does the government answer to—outside donors or its own citizens? That's the $10 billion question. When it came to the bottled water incident, then-President René Préval explained that he would love to stand up to the uninformed outsiders, but, as a weak state, Haiti had no choice but to grin and bear it—and ensure they didn't chase away the foreigners and their money.[105]

In many cases today, the state seems more interested in chasing aid than providing those institutions that will help ordinary Haitians. And because aid seeps into every fiber of the country's economy, plenty of ordinary Haitians respond, completely sensibly, in much the same shortsighted way. A job as a driver for a foreign NGO may only last for six or 12 or 18 months, until the group burns through its funding and pulls out. But it might be much more lucrative than any other option, often even for a Haitian with a decent education. It's little surprise, then, that aid focused on the coffee sector has yielded few hard or long-lasting results.

AID AND A LOSING CROP

"It's a losing crop for the small farmer," Marc Eddy Martin says of coffee.[106] "The coffee farmers, they are not coffee farmers. They plant coffee with other crops." Martin is a Haitian agronomist who directed the Coffee Center arm of Haiti's Ministry of Agriculture in the late 1970s. He also worked for USAID in Haiti for more than a decade, helping manage coffee projects into the '80s and '90s. "In an area where you have good co-ops, where a farmer can sell his coffee, they will maintain the coffee-producing tradition. But not in other areas, because the farmers, they are making more money with beans, yams, row crops, than coffee."

Under the Duvaliers, the Ministry of Agriculture funded agronomists and technicians who lived in rural areas and assisted farmers in the cultivation of all crops, including coffee. And coffee production remained relatively stable into the 1980s. Papa Doc also instituted a *Code du Café* in the late 1950s to govern every part of the supply chain, with the same totalitarian approach he used to govern every other aspect of the nation. Farmers could be fined, or even imprisoned, for bringing coffee that had stones or sticks mixed in to a local market, or that wasn't up to quality generally. The *Code* also formalized three distinct levels of the coffee chain: growers, licensed intermediaries known as *speculateurs*, and exporters. Research by some academics suggests that collusion among the traditional exporting families and the *speculateurs* who supplied them cut into small growers' profits. I've heard as much from plenty of Haitian old timers, who say that back then, the buying agents who collected coffee on behalf of *speculateurs* didn't dare cross the imaginary line that marked the limit between two of them, for fear of a punishment that would involve bodily harm of some sort.[107]

During the father-son reign, coffee remained a significant part of the economy. It accounted for 20 percent of export earnings into the 1980s and was the leading agricultural export, outpacing both cacao and mangoes. But despite outperforming other export crops, coffee had been on a gradual slide since the mid-20th century —it had accounted for over 65 percent of the value of all exports in 1955.[108] So USAID, working with the Haitian government, launched a series of projects that eventually snowballed into each other, with the overarching aim of increasing coffee production as a means to raise small farmers' incomes. The projects began as early as 1974 and lasted until 2009. They were known by various acronyms— PPC, PCC, CRP, HAP, MARCHE—and carried out by various aid contractors over the years. These were publicly funded endeavors, but plenty of private NGOs have launched similar coffee projects over the years, some spending millions of their own dollars in the process.[109]

The early USAID projects tried to bolster the sector by working alongside farmers on production, strengthening the cooperative system, and improving the country's coffee-processing capacity. Another major aim was to influence the government to modify the burdensome coffee export tax, a bill that was footed largely by poor rural growers and discouraged production. The tax remained as high as 26 percent of the export price into the late 1980s.[110] But the ultimate solution proposed for the sector, and the strategy that aid projects have been trying for more than 30 years, was an entirely new method: focus on washed coffee for export.

This has proven to be a successful strategy if executed properly. Rwanda, a country in sub-Saharan Africa that has nearly identically sized population, economy, land area, and coffee production as Haiti, is maybe the best example. In 2002, washed coffee accounted for just 1 percent of Rwandan production. By 2014, partly due to a big push by USAID, that share had ballooned to 42 percent. "When USAID built 120 washing stations in Rwanda," Michael Fairbanks says, "the Rwandans didn't think that this was a passing phase, because they had never received this kind of aid before. They took it more seriously."[111] Fairbanks, a consultant who has advised Rwandan President Paul Kagame for years and has consulted with Haitian leaders as well, points to that lack of aid saturation as a crucial distinction between Rwanda and Haiti.[112]

"We trained farmers for three years in coffee technology," Martin, the Haitian agronomist, says of one past USAID project he managed. The trainings covered how to produce new seedlings, prune trees properly, control leaf rust, and every other technical aspect of coffee production. The project spent $4.5 million from 1990-95 and produced more than 1 million seedlings.[113] But like all other coffee aid initiatives before and after, it couldn't stem the decline of the sector.

"The export market is practically dead for Haiti," says Martin, noting that nearly all the Haitian families who used to export coffee have exited the business. It probably didn't help that none of the exporters were very interested in the specialty washed coffee market in the U.S., the part of the industry that would soon begin to boom. "Exporters profess disinterest in handling the washed coffee from the Project," read another USAID report about the '90s project. "They do not think volumes will be large enough to interest them or that quality will be uniformly high. These exporters are used to marketing coffee as a commodity and do not have contacts in the specialty coffee trade."[114] It made sense—these exporters had traditionally focused on dry-processed coffee for European markets.

Today, Martin notes, most of the active coffee cooperatives in Haiti are viable only because of subsidies. He's especially aware of this fact because back in 1984, a USAID report that he co-wrote had noted: "Subsidies are probably necessary and should, therefore, not be ruled out for nascent cooperative organizations. However, subsidies should be extended to an organization only after a determination has been made of the conditions and timing necessary to eliminate them…" One problem with subsidies is that while plenty of people want to hand them out, almost no one ever follows through to take them away.

The unceasing aid still distorts incentives in Haiti's coffee sector. Practically all the infrastructure and equipment used by farmer cooperatives and associations were plopped down by an aid agency or NGO. Because nearly all these resources— washing stations, depulpers, even seedlings themselves—have been gifted, farmers have no equity in coffee ventures. The result is that there's no real ownership or accountability in many of the organizations that produce washed coffee for export today. And in turn, that means there are few incentives to make repairs when equipment fails, or to want to achieve long-term success generally.

Even for farmers who feel a real sense of ownership, almost none of the infrastructure built through these projects has been tailored to Haiti's context or needs. As a general rule, it's much too large for the low coffee yields and production levels in the country. Aid-funded wet mills are invariably massive concrete structures built in a style more suited for Central America, where farmers produce much greater volumes. These aid-built mills wind up operating at extremely low capacities and with consequently high labor, fuel, and water requirements. Most of them are so inefficient that they can't even break even—or at least they wouldn't be able to without support from outside aid groups. But the big concrete mills do make for nice photos in donor reports.

In Rwanda and elsewhere in East Africa, where coffee production much more closely mirrors Haiti's context than Central America does, TechnoServe and others have pushed micro wet mills appropriate for small quantities of coffee. Many of these mills use so-called "ecopulpers," innovative depulpers that remove the cherry's fruit and mucilage in one fell swoop and consequently use about 90 percent less water than traditional wet-process methods. TechnoServe also solved many of the lack of ownership issues because the micro-mill projects truly involved farmers, who gave structural materials like bamboo and rocks and earned sweat equity by providing labor.[115]

Over decades of aid projects, it seems that at some point, organizing as a co-op became not so much about producing the best possible coffee year after year, but instead a way to hang out a shingle and market to aid groups and NGOs. Economists call this sort of activity rent-seeking, which normally refers to spending resources chasing after political favors instead of on productive activity. The aid-seeking in Haiti's coffee sector is similar: cooperatives wind up chasing after seedlings, motorcycles, or grant funds on offer from aid groups, instead of trying to run a sustainable enterprise. And it's completely logical—much like a Haitian who decides his best option is to work as an NGO driver. If money is already earmarked for Haiti's coffee sector in a USAID budget, to take one example, then cooperatives would be silly not to go after it.

On top of these challenges, the staffs of many coffee co-ops and associations aren't necessarily qualified managers who are in charge because of merit. As the 1984 report put it: "Membership in cooperatives generally mirrors the distribution of power and resources in the local community. Thus, cooperative leadership is often made up of local elites."[116] Leaders might be in place simply because they're from the big family in town, and sometimes they veer into outright corruption, aiming to profit off of farmer members' production.

Despite the aid largesse over the years, Haiti's coffee sector remains in bad shape. Today, coffee accounts for less than 1 percent of the value of all exports, and it's fallen behind both cacao and mangoes.

Another measure that demonstrates the decline comes from a contrast between Haiti and Rwanda. Today, even though overall coffee production levels are nearly identical in the two countries, Rwandans earn about $60 million through coffee exports. Haitians earn just $2 million.[117]

Rwandans drink tea, though. Haitians drink coffee. In a way, Haitians choose to forgo some of those potential export earnings to keep more coffee at home. But it's exorbitantly expensive. Despite the fact that 90 percent of Haitian coffee is low-quality, the local prices for green coffee often rival the prices for higher-quality coffee on global markets. In fact, local prices have little to do with quality at all—high prices are simply the consequence of coffee becoming scarcer and scarcer after decades of farmers neglecting their plantings. The Haitian farmers who neglect coffee until harvest can still sell their meager volumes at what turns out to be a pretty decent price, given the low quality. It can be more straightforward, more profitable, and less risky to sell that low-quality product locally and get paid a little bit today, rather than take the extra effort to produce a high-quality product for export that might pay more, but with a six-month or longer lag time. The paradox, for me, is that local prices still haven't climbed high enough to spur many Haitian farmers to reinvest time and effort into production.

HAITI AGRICULTURAL PRODUCE EXPORT VALUES

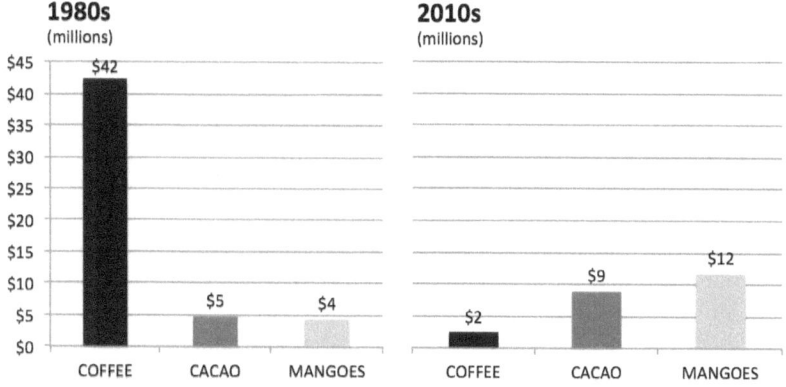

In the 1980s, the value of coffee exports exceeded $40 million, well ahead of the two next most-important agricultural products, cacao and mangoes. Today, coffee exports earn closer to $2 million and have fallen behind both other crops.[118]

Despite the high local price, most aid projects focus exclusively on the 5 percent of the sector that produces coffee for export. After all, talk of selling Haitian coffee in American cafes is sexy, and many donors want to fund projects that have a link back to their home countries. But for the most part, aid outsiders ignore the vast majority of the Haitian market that suggests coffee exports no longer make sense for many farmers.

Not only does it take relatively little time or attention to dry process a bad-quality coffee and sell it locally, but it also has an added advantage: farmers can store dry-processed coffee for months and then still sell it into the local market. Many farmers stock away a portion of coffee as a sort of rainy-day fund, or to pay kids' school fees next semester. When it comes to wet processing good-quality coffee for export markets, there are more steps and much higher costs. The model can make sense for some farmers, like those in Savane Zombie. But for farmers to justify the extra effort to participate in a cooperative and wash coffee for export, the price differential has to be worthwhile compared to the local price. The problem is that tacking on that export premium often drives the price to astronomical levels from the perspective of an international buyer.

Last year, for a little over $4.00 per pound an American roaster could have bought a Honduran coffee from the Cup of Excellence, a series of nationwide competitions and auctions that yield some of the most prized coffees in the world.[119] If that's the case, why would a roaster bother to buy from Haiti and deal with all the headaches and friction and red tape that come with any commerce there, just to pay the same $4.00 for a pound of decent-but-not-amazing coffee? The best reason may be the exclusivity angle.

Thompson Owen, the importer from Sweet Maria's, has written that when it comes to buying green coffee around the world, "there are some farms, some origins, some regions, that I simply don't have to re-evaluate constantly since I know they are incapable of producing great coffee." He included Cuba, Malaysia, China, Nepal, Venezuela, and Haiti on that list, which he made in 2004.[120] Around that time Chris Wade, a buyer at Coffee Bean International, in Portland, remembers "a lot of issues" appearing with the Haitian coffee his company bought from 1999-2008. The purchasing agreement was a direct result of one of the USAID projects from the series. "Coffee was regularly not on time as far as shipping," Wade told me. "You never knew when it would arrive, and you never knew what you were going to get."[121] The beans would be perfect one year, then "irregular and spongy" the next, and blanched completely white another. The quality was usually decent, he says, with cup scores of at least 80, but it swung significantly from year to year. Wade says that he wishes he could see Haitian coffee come back but that he would buy it again only "with extreme caution."

After tens of millions of dollars in aid spending, Haiti's sliding coffee production has yet to recover. And as some producers' forays into specialty markets show, they haven't mastered consistent quality control either—a deal-breaker for upscale coffee buyers today.

QUALITY, QUALITY, QUALITY

There's a thread of Haitian literature about urban elites dismissing peasants in the countryside as some combination of infantile, ridiculous, lazy, stupid, and superstitious—and doing so at their own peril. Much of the dismissing revolves around the peasants' adherence to Vodou, a religion that evolved during slavery and incorporated West African beliefs with aspects of Catholicism. One example is *The Beast of the Haitian Hills*, a short 1946 novel about a businessman from town who, after being widowed, moves to the country to take up farming alongside the peasants, who he considers ignorant and disrespectful. You can imagine where the story goes from there.

The authors were Philippe Thoby-Marcelin and Pierre Marcelin, brothers who had won much acclaim abroad for an earlier book, *Canapé-Vert*. The brothers noted, however, that the reception in Haiti was much different: disapproval and reprimand. Thoby-Marcelin explained their great sin: "…we had presented the life of peasants at grips with poverty and religious taboos instead of idealizing them or vindicating the upper class."[122]

It's easy to idealize the Haitian peasant. I've seen plenty of journalists do it, sometimes in reference to industrial developments that promise meager but steady wages and might provide some farmers with an opportunity beyond toiling in the soil under the tropical sun for 60 years. But it's probably just as easy to overcompensate and define rural Haitians by nothing but poverty.

Beyond quality or exclusivity, there's another reason that might spur some people to buy coffee from Haiti: you want to help Haitian smallholder farmers as much as humanly possible. There are a handful of well-intentioned, mostly

American groups that have bought coffee from Haitian cooperatives in recent years. And the buying strategy for most of them is simple: pay farmers as much as possible first and foremost, with quality concerns a clear second. These buyers aren't quality-driven coffee roasters; they're generally non-profit groups, and they often sell the coffee through church fundraisers or as part of a social mission. Some of these groups, particularly Wisconsin-based Singing Rooster, do grassroots work with coffee cooperatives all over Haiti, reinvest all revenues in the supply chain, and market a message of empowerment for small growers. But for others, the message winds up selling more pity than anything: buy coffee from Haiti to help the poor Haitian farmer. Their sentiments to help are laudable, but by divorcing quality incentives from price, they make it that much harder for specialty roasters to compete to buy coffee in Haiti. And if Haiti's coffee sector is going to revitalize itself, it will need more than a handful of well-intentioned charitable groups—it will need serious players in the coffee industry.

When it comes to specialty roasters, a coffee from Haiti does give you a unique origin story and might even add cachet to your menu. Direct trade, the model where roasters do their own due diligence about where beans come from, is largely about origin story, in addition to the focus on quality. And roasters like Intelligentsia, Counter Culture, and Stumptown pioneered direct trade partly because they weren't completely satisfied with its precursor: fair trade.[123]

Fair trade is really just a concept—treat the producer at the end of the supply chain well. It's a movement with roots in social justice. There are a handful of organizations that oversee fair-trade certification programs, and they strive to make the concept a reality through slightly different sets of standards. A fair-trade organization uses—and charges farmer groups for—its branded stamp to certify that produce adheres to its requirements.[124] In return, coffee farmers are guaranteed a minimum price, plus a "social premium" on top of that. The third-party stamp signals to customers that the grower has indeed been treated well—at least in theory, and insofar as the fair trade organization can tell. But the fair-trade label makes no claims regarding quality.[125]

Examples of fair-trade standards for producers include organizing as a cooperative with democratically elected leadership, using a portion of proceeds for community projects, and submitting to annual audits. Organic certifications are similar and can also yield price premiums for farmers, especially if they double-up with fair-trade certification. The organic requirements, however, have to do with things like not using chemical fertilizers or pesticides on your farm for at least the prior two years.[126]

From a farmer's perspective, the fair-trade message might be taken as: take a little detour from coffee production to jump through a series of somewhat-related hoops, and we'll give you a payoff in return. Direct trade's aim, on the other hand, is to tell farmers something more like: we're going to set a bar for you—maybe quite high—but it will be directly related to quality coffee. And if you clear the bar, then we'll compensate you handsomely.

A big part of the impetus for direct trade was the same desire to help growers that originated in fair-trade convictions. And the two aren't mutually exclusive—the same coffee can be certified direct-trade by a roaster and fair-trade by a third-party group. But given the coffee market's evolution toward quality, plus global internet adoption rates, direct trade may eventually make fair-trade labeling obsolete. If a small coffee grower in the mountains of a tropical country can use a cell phone to access a basic-HTML version of Facebook, or interact with an American roaster, then paying a third-party organization to handle that interaction via a label on a bag starts to feel outdated. And fair-trade groups may be realizing this themselves. While fair trade began as programs to certify bags of coffee, many of these organizations have evolved to the point that much of their current missions are to fund supply-chain projects and work with growers.[127]

Like many aspects of tropical supply chains, direct trade has weaknesses. Some coffee companies may be noble, honest, and able to do the diligence to figure out whether growers have actually been treated and paid well. Others might drift into simple P.R.-washing of their "coffee sourcing adventures," not really all that concerned about long-term and year-round relationships that span the beginnings and end of the supply chain.

There's a related issue between people at the opposite ends of the coffee chain that can seem a little like a temperate-tropical tug-of-war. When it comes to coffee, yields and crop performance in the field are what farmers see with their own eyes, and that's what they're likely to care about above all else. Most small coffee growers have never meticulously cupped coffee the way U.S. buyers do. Roasters, on the other hand, rightfully obsess over the quality of their product, often driven by that 85-point quality bar. Many of them therefore prefer the older coffee varieties—typica, bourbon, and their direct, unadulterated descendants. These heirloom varieties taste best in the cup but are susceptible to diseases on the farm and have extremely low yields compared to many newer cultivars.

Regardless of where you come out on this spectrum, the current situation in Haiti makes about as little sense as possible for everyone involved. There, 90 percent of the coffee is still typica, the low-yielding but potentially great-tasting variety, and 90 percent of the coffee is badly processed and bound for markets with few quality requirements. So for the vast majority of Haiti's coffee, the potential for excellent quality inherent to the beans is rendered irrelevant. It would only make sense to drastically shift those 90-percent figures in some way: either help farmers plant worse-tasting varieties with much better yields that can serve the local island market, or figure out a way to make high-quality typica coffee more viable for export. Haiti's case makes it easy to see why small growers and quality-driven buyers can wind up with very different viewpoints when it comes to questions about the coffee chain.

Along that chain one of the aims wrapped up in direct trade—helping growers —turns out to be a flat-out difficult proposition, even with a company known for setting trends in producer-roaster relations. "How does a grower fare differently in one of these price-premium receiving scenarios?" asked Kim Elena Ionescu, a former Counter Culture coffee buyer who now works for the SCAA, specialty coffee's industry group, in a 2013 talk. "Is there a connection between the quality of a grower's coffee and the quality of her life?"[128] If only a small portion of her coffee qualifies, Ionescu said, then a quality premium will never be able to transform her livelihood—figuring out how to increase volume should probably be her main concern instead. A 2012 Counter Culture report noted another issue with paying quality premiums: the scheme confused some cooperative members in Peru, who saw "their neighbors receive a higher price while using what appear to be the same techniques they are using in cultivation and post-cultivation." Other farmers would earn a premium one year, but not the next, and not understand why. From a grower's perspective, the whole thing could seem like a lottery.[129]

But Counter Culture, like other companies in the vanguard of direct trade, keeps evolving—and improving its models. A more recent report notes that its quality premiums are helping growers in southern Colombia to reinvest in coffee production, and it identified eight key practices farmers can use that correlate to earning premiums in repeated years.[130] Winston Harrison, the roaster in Nashville, describes his company's buying approach this way: "We assume that by producing coffee to the best of your ability you are taking great care of your land, and we pay a premium price, which is usually above fair trade price and commodity market rates." He adds that they always want to be able to trace a coffee all the way back to the farm level, "especially if we are hoping to establish a relationship for years to come. The quality and the direct relationship are most important to us."

As the industry and its supply chain continue to evolve, aid will continue to overlap with the coffee sector around the globe. Coffee necessarily creates a link between growers in the tropical world and drinkers in countries that give aid. In Haiti, the dynamics between the global coffee sector, local markets, and food production have made coffee a losing proposition for many small farmers. These factors have hamstrung the export sector and doomed many of the aid projects related to coffee. So in light of the challenges, why agree to spend 12 more months in the country working in that sector?

AVOIDING AID PITFALLS

"Although some temporary increases in production were recorded," the 1984 USAID report on coffee revitalization efforts reads, "...the project was not able to halt the steady decrease in coffee production that has afflicted Haiti for the last 30 years. The elaborate input, extension, and credit delivery mechanisms of this project did not function well during its life and ceased functioning altogether once AID financing was withdrawn."[131]

Pretty much everything we've tried to do with the Haiti Coffee Academy has been tried before—after decades and millions of dollars of aid projects, there's not much new left to try. But sometimes the way you approach an endeavor can be just as important as what you're trying to accomplish. And we tried to structure operations in a way that avoids many of the traditional pitfalls of aid, at least to the extent that's possible for any organization working in the wider aid landscape in Haiti.

The Haiti Coffee Academy is a registered agricultural business—it's a company, not an NGO. It's definitely a business with a social mission, one that few investors whose major concern was a hefty or quick return would choose to back. But the structure meant that the attitude from the get-go was that it had to be self-sustaining, ultimately. The strategy to make it financially sustainable is to take a small margin from the revenues that come from sales of Haitian coffee and pump it back into the business, and into more efforts to improve production on the ground. The viability of the plan will ultimately depend on increasing production.

A 30-hectare demonstration farm and nursery is the hub. The farmland had sat abandoned for about 25 years, the eight heirs of the family patriarch long gone to Philadelphia and other places abroad. When I first saw it, it was what Haitians call a *rak*—a jungle—overgrown with wild vegetation that choked decrepit, rust-infested coffee trees.

Over summer and fall of 2014, we replanted the farm with more than 20,000 coffee plants that we'd raised from seed. The farm staff uses traditional methods—organic fertilizers, hand tools, natural pesticides—for virtually everything, the idea being that any smallholder in Haiti could replicate the methods used on the farm if they wanted to. At the nursery, which produces between 30,000 and 50,000 seedlings each year, staff tests different coffee varieties to see how they perform in the field and, eventually, in the cup. We've propagated traditional Haitian typica coffee, as well as five varieties from Brazil, along with one from Colombia. Once the trees have matured and the farm has come into production, workers will use an efficient and modern Penagos-made ecopulper to process coffee.

The essence of the initiative, however, is the work with smallholder farmers across the region. In fall of 2014, we started a training program in basic coffee-growing techniques with about 350 families in the area. The aim is to help interested farmers increase the quantity and quality of their coffee—and ultimately improve their livelihoods. The trainings are modeled after ones that TechnoServe has used in East Africa to help some farmers increase their yields by 50-100 percent over two to three years. They're extremely practical—for the dozen training groups, the coffee farm is the classroom, and trainings are very hands-on. Farmers learn by doing, by applying different growing techniques on a small demonstration plot that each group has dedicated to the purpose. The trainings are designed for adults who might not be literate and might have little or no formal education, and they're entirely in Haitian Creole.[132]

Most of the subject matter covers the same coffee-growing topics that aid projects have been covering for years. Whether the work succeeds will mostly likely come down to two simple things: management and execution. Truly forming relationships and building trust with coffee farmers, rather than just a board of local elites who run a cooperative, goes a long way. One of the modules in the training program had little to do with coffee production at all, at least not directly —it was on gender equality. After the gender unit's month, Madame Didier, one of our trainers, told me that it was a hit with each of the four training groups that she leads. One group requested that they go over the module again, only this time they wanted to do it at church one Sunday, so that other members of their community could participate. I don't know how much our work will ultimately succeed, but I know that farmers lobbying to do training modules during church is probably a good sign of local buy-in.

The Academy essentially gives away nothing beyond the training. When it comes to nurseries, for instance, we have not built one of them for farmers—we've built about a dozen of them with farmers. They provided the labor, land, water, and tools, and we provided the agronomic know-how and access to seed. Ultimately, they'll be able to replant their aging coffee trees little by little.

It costs nothing beyond farmers' time to attend trainings. But the goal is to have participants who see the value in the knowledge, not people who show up to a meeting because they think they'll get a free lunch. And I mean that literally. As we established the training groups, another of our trainers said that at one initial meeting a group had protested—been in disbelief, really—that lunch wouldn't be offered during trainings. They said that a two-hour session that doesn't include a meal was unheard of. We said that we weren't an NGO. The group wound up giving our trainer so many problems that we decided to disband it. We preferred to spend our time and energy working with farmers who were on the same page. Fortunately, the initiative's backers felt the same way—they were more interested in supporting meaningful work than in touting inflated figures about the number of participants, a hang-up for many aid donors.

Perhaps the most important factor of all is the connection to markets that actually reward farmers' extra effort toward quality. Slowly but surely, we've seen some progress. The Savan Zombi coffee that was released by La Colombe in summer 2015 came out of a new buying relationship formed by Cantave and me. The farmers who produced it were already organized into their own coffee association, and they now also participate in the Haiti Coffee Academy training program. It was a small amount, but it turned out to be the best quality coffee La Colombe had ever bought from Haiti.[133] Since then, additional American roasters have shown interest in buying Haitian coffee and supporting our work on the ground. Allegro, the coffee arm of Whole Foods, purchased a small order from the same farmer group in 2016.

It doesn't happen overnight. Coffee is a tree crop that takes up to four years to give its first full harvest. It's definitely a long-term outlook and effort.

Part of the appeal to me was the schedule of the plan. The idea was to turn over complete day-to-day management to local staff as quickly as possible, which we did in the fall of 2015. A lot of aid groups in Haiti and around the world have been talking about "working themselves out of jobs" for decades, still with no end in sight. In Senegal, this was something fellow Peace Corps Volunteers and I joked about anytime a staff member recited that line—the program was established in the country in 1962. I didn't just want to earn my keep as an expat working in Haiti, I wanted it to be a temporary setup. Given the year or so of prior work done to lay the Academy's foundations, Cantave and I figured that if we couldn't get things set up in 12 months, it might never be able stand on its own anyway.

Recently, after someone asked me to explain a little bit about the venture and approach, they asked me a simple question: Will it work? I can't say for sure. There are so many fundamental challenges about Haiti and its coffee sector that it obviously won't be it easy. At times, I've wondered whether just giving farmers cash instead of spending it on a coffee initiative would do more good for them. Organizations like GiveDirectly have pioneered this sort of approach, and I'd be lying if I said that I didn't sometimes still wonder about it. I answered that it will come down to production. If we can help farmers increase their coffee production and get their costs down, then it has a chance. But it all hinges on one thing: making coffee work for small-scale Haitian farmers.

5

CONCLUSION

WILL IT WORK?

"WILL HAITI WORK?" Anténor Firmin, the astute Foreign Affairs Minister, asked in 1905. He was wondering how Haiti would fit in with the reality that the United States had emerged as the major power in the region.[134] People had been asking versions of that question for 100 years before Firmin. They've now been asking it for 100 years after. They'll probably be asking it for a long time to come.

It seems to me that Haiti does work—at least it works about exactly the way you'd expect it to given the political and economic institutions that affect everyday life there, the historical foundations of the place, and the effects of seemingly perpetual aid that has saturated the country. And you could argue that it works extraordinarily well when it comes to the one thing it seems set up to do above all else: preserve power for a small slice of the population.

A recent report by the World Bank noted that many of the same old elite families from the Duvaliers' reign "remain in control of large segments of the economy today," 30 years after their ouster. Because these industries are highly concentrated, there's little competition within them, which has caused entire segments of the economy to ossify. The salient exception is in telecommunications, where the cell and wireless internet provider Digicel has transformed the country and its connectivity. In 2005, the year Digicel obtained its license to operate in Haiti, there were 500,000 cellular subscriptions. Today there are nearly 7 million.[135] The transformation took the backing of a bullheaded Irish billionaire CEO who was bound and determined to overhaul the status quo, regardless of how many people he upset in government or industry. Most of Haiti's economy, by contrast, has become immune to the innovations and disruptions that competition spurs. The same World Bank report estimated that for food products sold in highly concentrated markets, prices in Haiti are 30–60 percent higher than in other countries in the region.[136]

Two centuries of concentrated and near-unchecked power have left their marks. The legacy now shows up in the friction you encounter everywhere in Haiti. I was talking to a Haitian businessman about this one day, airing my frustrations that seemingly no matter where you went—a business like a bank or hotel, or a government office, or anywhere else—it was as if you had to have a letter signed by the King himself to get any little thing done. The businessman provided a simple explanation: people are still conditioned to dictatorship. Everyone is afraid to give authorization for anything, he said, because if you did that back in the day and made the wrong decision, you'd "get your head chopped off." I don't think he was being literal, but I'd have believed him if he were.

Unfortunately, much of the foreign aid to Haiti has reinforced the institutions that work for the power brokers and against the people. In today's dollar terms, USAID gave the equivalent of $1.2 billion in aid to Baby Doc during his rule, from 1971-86. Duvalier pocketed much of the money, as he did with foreign aid from other sources. A 1980 IMF grant gave $22 million to Haiti; from it, an estimated $4 million funded the Tonton Makout, while $16 million disappeared into the president's own personal accounts.[137]

Why does the U.S. government send all that aid, whether to Haiti or elsewhere? If aid were fundamentally based on need, you might expect the top recipients to be in sub-Saharan Africa, home to some of the poorest countries in the world. In reality, geopolitical factors usually trump need—Israel, Egypt, and Pakistan routinely top the list of biggest recipients of U.S. aid. When it came to Papa Doc's Haiti, part of the impetus to send aid to the dictator was political: he masterfully played up Cold War-era fears about the need for a bulwark against Castro and his communists an island away.[138]

Political concerns don't just alter where aid goes, they can also influence how much of it goes to a particular country from year-to-year. The State Department and the wider U.S. government seem to have one simple and overarching policy goal toward Haiti: stability. Senator Marco Rubio spoke frankly about the topic during a 2015 hearing: "When Haiti is stable and prosperous, America benefits. When Haiti is unstable, unsecure and lacking in opportunity for its people, it creates vacuums where criminal gangs—or worse—can operate. And it can lead to migratory pressures in the U.S.—or disastrous and deadly tragedies on the high seas."[139] Rubio's last comment hearkened back to the early 1990s, when tens of thousands of Haitians fled for the States on rickety boats. The refugees were tying to escape economic disaster brought about by years of international sanctions. The measures aimed to punish a military junta that had taken power in a 1991 coup, but they primarily punished the masses. In late 1994, then-President Bill Clinton told the American people that without action, "We will continue to face the threat of a mass exodus of refugees and its constant threat to stability in our region and control of our borders."[140] The next year, in 1995, USAID's aid to Haiti shot up by 59 percent, before returning to pre-boat-exodus levels the following year. It's hard to deny that one aim of using government aid to lessen Haiti's problems is to minimize the United States' own problems.[141]

In recent decades, the tens of millions of aid dollars funneled into the coffee sector have left little in the way of progress for farmers across the Haitian countryside. One reason is that people have misunderstood the underpinnings of the country, much as they did when the people uprooted Duvalier. Haiti's unending transition to democracy persists because the country didn't just need a new regime, it needed a new form of government to replace its historical dictatorship. The aid saturation in Haiti is similar. It won't matter much what the acronym of the latest coffee project is, or which aid contractor carries it out, because the country doesn't just need a new project, it needs a new model to replace its current aid-government system. Until that happens, training small-scale coffee farmers can only be expected to accomplish so much.

When it comes to coffee, you could ask a similar question about the future of the entire industry: Will coffee work? Haiti may just be a canary in the coal mine. Coffee farmers around the world, particularly the 25 million of them who are smallholders, face many of the same issues that Haitians do. Climate change is shifting the limits of the tropical belt where coffee is viable, with its growing range retreating up mountain slopes. Recent research suggests that the global area suitable for coffee could fall by half by 2050.[142] These changes will only exacerbate existing issues in the sector, like drought and leaf rust. In addition, many of the world's coffee farmers are nearing 60 or 70 years of age, and it's uncertain as to whether the generation that follows will want to stick to farming. More and more growers are leaving coffee farms to search for better economic opportunities in cities, particularly in Latin America. And producers face sustainability concerns all over coffee-growing Africa, where socio-economic conditions and small-scale agricultural methods are similar to those in Haiti. In the mid 1960s, African countries produced more than 19 million bags of coffee; by the end of the 1980s, that had fallen to 16 million. Over the same period, Africa's contribution to global coffee production fell from 25 percent to just 12 percent.[143]

But where there's challenge, there's opportunity. Exploding demand for better coffee shows no signs of stopping, and smallholders like those across Haiti or Africa —who will never be able to compete with large estates on volume—may be best positioned to take advantage. Specialty coffee now accounts for half of demand in the U.S., the second-largest market in the world. In Europe, collectively the world's biggest market, good coffee is also finally catching on, where some 40 percent of it is now specialty. And growth is booming in traditionally tea-drinking China too, where Starbucks plans to open more than one cafe a day over the next three years.[144]

African producers see the promise coffee offers, and some have already started to benefit, with Rwanda a prime example. Continent-wide, nearly 30 percent of coffee production is now specialty, up from less than 15 percent three years ago. "These approaches that focus on farmer profitability are the only way to sustain the industry" Abdullah Bagersh, chairman of the African Fine Coffee Association, told *The Wall Street Journal* in early 2016. "With quality beans, African farmers have a competitive advantage."[145]

That same opportunity exists in Haiti, despite the challenges presented by the wider political and economic environments there. The dynamics of the local coffee market are bound to change sooner than later—it makes little sense for Haitians with an average annual income of $820, just one-tenth of the Latin American average, to pay higher prices for worse coffee than other countries in the region. Even a country like Colombia, the third-largest producer in the world and with a per capita income nearly eight times that of Haiti, has traditionally bought cheaper beans from Ecuador and Peru to satisfy local demand. That allows their farmers to export most of their own coffee at higher prices, and earn more income on balance.[146] If local prices in Haiti come back down to more realistic levels one day, then farmers stand a better chance of decreasing their costs and making for-export coffee much more feasible.[147] But the growers have to be prepared for that day—and see an incentive to stick with coffee. If not, then one day there truly may be no coffee farmers left in Haiti.

The issues that extend far beyond the local coffee dynamics present tougher obstacles. While the market dynamics seem likely to change, no one can say how long the transition to democracy will remain in its interminable state. Despite the uncertainty, and the fact that living in Haiti could wear on me at times, I'm still a big believer that small improvements in many areas can make big differences in families' lives and livelihoods. Maybe an undying streak of chastened idealism is a given for someone who studied economics and served in the Peace Corps. But that's the aim we've tried to take with the Haiti Coffee Academy, and that's the type of approach that has a chance to help ordinary Haitians improve their own livelihoods.

Watson Reby, 11, is just one of the younger siblings of our farm employee, Sonord. I have an image of Watson seared into my mind: him standing in his uniform ready for school, head freshly shaved. His tiny frame and pencil-thin waist made me wonder whether any rural Haitian children would fall into the typical range on the height-weight charts at the doctor's office. Sonord's work helps pay Watson's school fees, and since their father died, his steady job is even more important for the family. When we replanted the farm in 2014, Watson came around just about every day after school to watch us pull the small bagged trees out of the nursery and transport them for planting. He would tell me how much he loves school—and I have a feeling that he meant it in a way that an 11-year-old American might not have, because every school-going Haitian child I've ever talked to has told me how much they love it. It must sure beat fetching five gallons of water on your head or doing whatever other household chores you'd be doing if at home during the day.

Watson also liked to learn about what we were doing on the farm, and Cantave was always quick to explain different basics about coffee agronomy to him, or why we would follow a certain technique, like taking care to cradle the root system while slicing open a bagged seedling to plant it. Sonord didn't have the chance to stay in school long enough to graduate, but maybe his younger brother will. Maybe he'll use that education as a springboard to go onto bigger things. Maybe he'll want to become a coffee agronomist one day. I just hope that if that day does come, Haiti will work for him.

ACKNOWLEDGEMENTS

SINCE WE MET in 2013, Cantave Fils-Aimé has always been a good-spirited cultural, linguistic, and agronomic guide to his country. I'm grateful for his friendship, and for the rest of the Haiti Coffee Academy staff—in particular, Rousseau Gabriel, Smith Bazil, Sonord Reby, Rodrigue Bazile, Markenzy Estriplet, Jean Baptiste Bazile, and Mistral Jean Louis. Among many other things, they always made me feel welcome in their corner of rural Haiti, and they always called me by my name.

I'm also thankful for Conor Murphy, who laid the foundations of the Haiti Coffee Academy, never failed to pack freshly roasted coffee when visiting, and insisted that Haiti didn't need another NGO, at least not when it came to this venture. I'm grateful for Isabelle Lagarde, too, as she was instrumental in the beginnings of our coffee efforts in Haiti and understood the challenges of working with each foot in a different world. I also thank Carl Cervone and his years of coffee experience, which helped me start to make sense of an informal, fragmented, and often opaque supply chain.

Publishing this account marks the end of a five-year chapter of my life mostly lived in Haiti, much of it spent trying to grapple with the issues that cover the preceding pages. Over those years, many friends and colleagues have shared countless conversations with me about Haiti, coffee, aid, and much more. All of them have helped shape this account in one way or another, and I especially thank Jacob Kushner, Peter Granitz, Isaac Gardner, Nicole Phillips, Ana Adamson, Junior Verna, Rob Johnson, Richard Haspil, Douglas Wiener, Jon Bougher, and Edwin Ceide.

Laurent Dubois' book about the Haitian Revolution, *Avengers of the New World*, is the first book about Haiti that I remember ever picking up. His writings have helped me immensely when it comes to trying to make sense of the place today, and when it came to crafting the historical sections of this account. I thank him for that, and for his comments on an early draft.

I thank Jennifer Zambone for graciously editing and commenting on various drafts. I also thank Don Davis and Tyler Cowen for helpful comments on early drafts.

Finally, I thank my mom, Barbara Watkins, for being my first editor, and for passing on a sense of wonder about the world.

ABOUT THE AUTHOR

TATE WATKINS is an economics researcher, writer, and editor. He worked in the Haitian coffee sector for two years with TechnoServe and the Haiti Coffee Academy. Prior to that, he spent two years as a freelance journalist in Haiti reporting on economic development, foreign aid, and immigration for a variety of print and web outlets. Watkins earned M.A. and B.A. degrees in economics from Clemson University and served in the Peace Corps in Senegal. He lives in Greenville, South Carolina.

NOTES

1. The description of James Franklin comes from the preface to the 1971 edition of his book, *The Present State of Haiti (Saint Domingo), 1828: With Remarks on its Agriculture, Commerce, Laws Religion etc.* 1971. His description of the coffee plantation comes from p. 352-353.

2. According to Haiti's National Coffee Institute, the average yield in the country is 200-240 kilograms of green coffee per hectare. The Central American average is 605 kilograms per hectare, according to FAOSTAT data.

3. Association National del Café. Departamento de Comercialización de Anacafé: Ingreso de divisas.

4. Institut National du Café d'Haïti. "Actualisation du diagnostic de la filière café en Haïti." Draft version. 2013.

5. International Fund for Agricultural Development. "Enabling the rural poor to overcome poverty in Haiti." 2008.

6. Franklin. *The Present State of Haiti (Saint Domingo), 1828: With Remarks on its Agriculture, Commerce, Laws Religion etc.* 1971. p. 352.

7. Charlie Papazian describes the evolution of the U.S. beer industry in *The Complete Joy of Homebrewing*. 2003.

8. Steve Hindy documents the rise of craft beer in *The Craft Beer Revolution: How a Band of Microbrewers Is Transforming the World's Favorite Drink*. 2015.

9. Data on craft beer come from the Brewer's Association: National Beer Sales and Production Data. Philip H. Howard describes shifting dynamics of the U.S. beer market in "Beer behemoths struggle to fend off craft brew craze." *The Conversation*. September 29, 2015.

10. References to the growth and size of coffee market segments draw from Daniele Giovannucci, "Sustainable Coffee Survey of the North American Specialty Coffee Industry," 2001; as well as the Specialty Coffee Association of America: U.S. Specialty Coffee Facts & Figures, December 2015.

11. Mark Pendergrast describes the 20th-century U.S. coffee market in Bitter Brews, Part Three of *Uncommon Grounds: The History of Coffee and How It Transformed Our World*. 2010. "Coffee Consumption Over the Last Century," by Jean C. Buzby and Stephen Haley, of the USDA Economic Research Service, describes historical U.S. coffee consumption. June 1, 2007.

12. USDA Economic Research Service. Coffee, tea, and cocoa: Per capita availability. Data converted to six-ounce cups.

13. Loxcel Geomatics: How many Starbucks are there? January 2016.

14. Pendergrast. *Uncommon Grounds: The History of Coffee and How It Transformed Our World.* 2010. p. 281.

15. Much of the background on Peet, Knutsen, and the evolution of the coffee market comes from "Romancing the Bean," Part Four of Pendergrast's book. *Uncommon Grounds: The History of Coffee and How It Transformed Our World.* 2010.

16. Some coffee companies use terms like "relationship coffee" or phrases like "We shake the hand of the farmer," in addition to or instead of "direct trade"—they are synonymous for the most part. In *The New Yorker*, Kelefa Sanneh writes about modern coffee evangelists and the rise of high-quality coffee. "Sacred Grounds: Aida Batlle and the new coffee evangelists." November 21, 2011. Michaele Weissman's 2008 book, *God in a Cup: The Obsessive Quest for the Perfect Coffee*, profiles some of the same coffee professionals in more depth.

17. Direct trade and fair trade aren't mutually exclusive—the same coffee can be simultaneously certified fair-trade by a third-party organization and certified direct-trade by a coffee company.

18. For more detail on Starbucks' Coffee and Farmer Equity (C.A.F.E.) practices, see the company's "Global Responsibility Report 2014: What is the Role and Responsibility of a For-Profit Public Company?"

19. For much of this segment of the coffee industry, the transparency component of direct trade has a specific meaning: every party in the supply chain, from grower to exporter to importer to roaster, knows who is getting paid how much. The description about Stumptown's purchasing comes from the company website: Stumptown Coffee Roasters: Our Story: What does Direct Trade mean to Stumptown? Background on Counter Culture Coffee's buying ethos comes from two sources from its website: "Counter Culture Direct Trade Certification!" May 19, 2008; and Sustain: What We Are Doing: Purchasing Principles. The Geoff Watts quote comes from an interview by Shanna Germain for *The Specialty Coffee Chronicle*: "Direct Trade: Going Straight to the Source." February 14, 2012.

20. A green coffee price is a crude measure for gauging effects at the farm level because it's simply the final export price—the amount of money that stays within the growing country. That amount lumps together all costs from the multiple levels of the supply chain, from a rural grower to an urban shipping port. And how those costs break down—including what percentage of the export price a farmer receives—can vary wildly between coffee-producing countries. When it comes to those green coffee prices, importers and roasters usually talk in terms of "F.O.B.," a shipping designation that stands for "free on board" and generally equates to the price up to point of export. F.O.B. designates when and where a seller transfers ownership of goods to a buyer, which traditionally happened once cargo passed over a ship's rail as it was loaded.

21. The French "th" sound in "Thiotte" is pronounced like an English "ch" sound. In English, the phonetic spelling for the town is something like: "Chut."

22. USDA Foreign Agricultural Service: Production, Supply, and Distribution Online.

23. Hawaii does produce a marginal amount of coffee—about 0.03 percent of the world's total, according to USDA Foreign Agricultural Service data.

24. Background on arabica and canephora draws on R.J. Clarke and R. Macrae. *Coffee: Volume 1: Chemistry.* 1985. The ideal temperature range for most coffee plants is 60-80° F. The arabica species needs a minimum of about 1,500 millimeters of rainfall per year and relative humidity of about 60-70 percent.

25. Description of coffee's origins and cultivation draw from

William H. Ukers, *All About Coffee*, 1922; John M. Talbot, *Grounds for Agreement: The Political Economy of the Coffee Commodity Chain*, 2004; as well as Clarke and Macrae's book, *Coffee: Volume 1: Chemistry.* 1985.

26. Haiti's National Coffee Institute reports that 90 percent of the country's coffee is the typica

variety. Technically, a variety is a sub-group of a species that occurred from a natural mutation; a cultivar is a sub-group that humans created by crossing two different plants of the same species. A hybrid is created by crossing two different plants of two different species. The word "varietal" is sometimes used interchangeably with variety; it was created by the wine industry as a marketing term.

27. Carrie Kahn. "Rust Devastates Guatemala's Prime Coffee Crop And Its Farmers." NPR. July 28, 2014.

28. The estimate for the number of smallholder coffee farmers worldwide comes from the Fairtrade Foundation. Data on Haiti's smallholders come from Institut National du Café d'Haïti. "Actualisation du diagnostic de la filière café en Haïti." Draft version. October 2013.

29. One bag equals 60 kilograms of green coffee, roughly 132 pounds. Data come from USDA Foreign Agricultural Service: Production, Supply, and Distribution Online.

30. Commodity prices come from the Intercontinental Exchange: Coffee C Futures. Transparent Trade Coffee, a project at the Goizueta Business School at Emory University, routinely gathers price data on high-end coffee.

31. Zora Neale Hurston. *Tell My Horse: Voodoo and Life in Haiti and Jamaica*. Chapter 7: The Next Hundred Years. 1938.

32. Various demographic data for Haiti come from the World Bank and UNICEF. The figure about Haitian migrants in the United States comes from "Income per Natural: Measuring Development for People Rather Than Places," by Michael A. Clemens and Lant Pritchett. *Population and Development Review*. September 2008. See also: "Let the People Go: The Problem with Strict Migration Limits, " by Michael Clemens and Justin Sandefur. *Foreign Affairs*. January/February 2014.

33. For instance: "Where the World's Coffee Comes From." *BloombergBusinessweek*. February 13, 2014.

34. The excellent overview of Haitian history by Laurent Dubois, *Haiti: The Aftershocks of History*, published in 2012, provides much of the background for this section and chapter.

35. Dubois notes the magnitudes of Saint Domingue's sugar and coffee production, as well as the value of the colony relative to British ones. *Haiti: The Aftershocks of History*. 2012. p. 18. David Eltis' research demonstrates that the colony had become the richest society in the world. *General History of the Caribbean, Volume 3*. "The slave economies of the Caribbean: Structure, performance, evolution and significance." 1997. p. 105-137.

36. Robin Blackburn documents the beginning of the slave trade in the Caribbean in *The Making of New World Slavery: From the Baroque to the Modern, 1492-1800*. 1997. p. 137. Elizabeth Abbott describes slaves' living conditions in *Haiti: A Shattered Nation*. 2011. p. 30.

37. Michel-Rolph Trouillot describes the relationship between the cultivation of sugar and coffee in "Motion in the System: Coffee, Color, and Slavery in Eighteenth-Century Saint-Domingue." 1982. He also cites Terrier-Rouge as the place coffee was introduced. "Motion in the System." 1982. p. 349.

38. Trouillot. "Motion in the System." 1982. p. 348.

39. Georges Anglade. *Atlas Critique d'Haïti*. 1982. p. 37.

40. Dubois describes the *affranchis* in *Avengers of the New World: The Story of the Haitian Revolution*. 2004. p. 61. In "Motion in the System," Trouillot describes the coffee plantations of the *affranchis* class. Sidney W. Mintz provides related background in "Can Haiti Change?" *Foreign Affairs*. January/February 1995.

41. The census figures are as cited by Dubois in *Haiti: The Aftershocks of History*. 2012. p. 19. The original estimates come from Moreau de Saint-Méry. *Description topographique, physique, civile, politique et historique de la partie française de l'isle Saint-Domingue*. 1797. Dubois documents the revolutionary period in detail in *Avengers of the New World: The Story of the Haitian Revolution*. 2004.

42. David Geggus documents the origins of the country's name in "The Naming of Haiti." *New West Indian Guide*. 1997. According to the FAO, 63 percent of Haiti's land area has slopes 20 percent or steeper. Natural Resources Management and Environment Department. Land Resources Information

Systems in the Caribbean: Haiti. 2000.

43. Dubois. *Haiti: The Aftershocks of History*. 2012. p. 94

44. Anglade. *Atlas Critique d'Haïti*. 1982. p. 31.

45. Gerald Francis Murray describes rural agricultural practices in "Evolution of Haitian Peasant Land Tenure: A Case Study in Agrarian Adaptation to Population Growth." 1977. p. 210.

46. William Gervase, Clarence-Smith, and Steven Topik. *The Global Coffee Economy in Africa, Asia, and Latin America, 1500–1989*. Appendix: Historical Statistics of Coffee Production and Trade from 1700 to 1960. 2006.

47. Mark Pendergrast describes Brazil's coffee production history in "The Coffee Kingdoms" section of *Uncommon Grounds*. 2010.

48. Dubois. *Haiti: The Aftershocks of History*. 2012. p. 103.

49. Victor Schoelcher. *Colonies étrangères et Haïti: résultats de l'émancipation anglaise*. 1843. p. 198.

50. Richard A. Haggerty. "Haiti: A Country Study." Government Printing Office for the Library of Congress. 1989.

51. Population figures come from Schoelcher in *Colonies étrangères et Haïti*, 1843; and Benoit Joachim, *Les racines du sous développement en Haïti*. 1979.

52. Glenn R. Smucker et al. USAID. "Environmental Vulnerability in Haiti: Findings and Recommendations." 2007. p. 17.

53. Jean André Victor. "Une agriculture résiliente face aux crises et aux chocs: le cas d'Haïti. La résilience de l'agriculture Haïtienne face aux chocs provoqués par l'homme et les catastrophes naturelles." 2013. p. 37.

54. Mats Lundahl. "Population Pressure and Agrarian Property Rights in Haiti." 1980. p 279.

55. Lundahl outlines the underlying pressures that have resulted in deforestation of much of the country in *Poverty in Haiti: Essays on Underdevelopment and Post Disaster Prospects*. 2010. p. 32. Remy N. Bargout and Manish N. Raizada discuss declining soil fertility in "Soil nutrient management in Haiti, pre-Columbus to the present day: lessons for future agricultural interventions." *Agriculture & Food Security*. 2013. Data on declining cereal yields per hectare over time can be found from the World Bank.

56. Michel-Rolph Trouillot. *Haiti: State Against Nation*. 1990. p. 61.

57. Dubois. *Haiti: The Aftershocks of History*. 2012. p. 116.

58. Lincoln and his advisors actually concocted a half-baked plan to send slaves from the American South to Haiti. They sent 453 freed slaves to Ile-à-Vache before abandoning the idea. For more background, see James D. Lockett. "Abraham Lincoln and Colonization: An Episode That Ends in Tragedy at L'Ile a Vache, Haiti, 1863-1864." *Journal of Black Studies*. 1991.

59. Peter James Hudson. "Where Does Haiti Fit in Citigroup's Corporate History?" *BloombergView*. June 13, 2012.

60. A few years prior, in 1912, the Secretary of State demonstrated his somewhat-limited understanding of Haiti. Upon learning some basic facts about the country in a background meeting, he said: "Think of it! Niggers speaking French!" Laurent Dubois. *Haiti: The Aftershocks of History*. 2012. p. 212.

61. Haggerty. "Haiti: A Country Study." Government Printing Office for the Library of Congress. 1989.

62. Trouillot. *Haiti: State Against Nation*. 1990. p. 183.

63. Detail about Haiti's manufacturing industry and it history draws from Lundahl. *Poverty in Haiti: Essays on Underdevelopment and Post Disaster Prospects*. 2010. p. 168, 197; as well as Haggerty, "Haiti: A Country Study." Government Printing Office for the Library of Congress. 1989.

64. Haggerty. "Haiti: A Country Study." Government Printing Office for the Library of Congress. 1989.

65. Trouillot. *Haiti: State Against Nation*. 1990. p. 211.

66. Raju Jan Singh and Mary Barton-Dock provide detail on agriculture and food imports. World Bank. "Haiti—Toward a new narrative: systematic country diagnostic." 2015. p. 28. Maura R. O'Connor

reports on rice policy. "Subsidizing Starvation: How American tax dollars are keeping Arkansas rice growers fat on the farm and starving millions of Haitians." *Foreign Policy*. January 11, 2013.

67. United Nations Statistics Division. Demographic Yearbook 2014.

68. Laura Jaramillo and Cemile Sancak. International Monetary Fund. "Growth in the Dominican Republic and Haiti: Why has the Grass Been Greener on One Side of Hispaniola?" 2007.

69. Haggerty. "Haiti: A Country Study." Government Printing Office for the Library of Congress. 1989.

70. Haggerty. "Haiti: A Country Study." Government Printing Office for the Library of Congress. 1989.

71. Lundahl. *Poverty in Haiti: Essays on Underdevelopment and Post Disaster Prospects*. 2010. p. 35; and Lundahl. Inter-American Development Bank. "Sources of Growth in the Haitian Economy." 2004.

72. One bag equals 60 kilograms of green coffee, roughly 132 pounds. Sources for historical coffee export data for Saint Domingue and Haiti include: James Franklin. *The Present State of Haiti (Saint Domingo), 1828: With Remarks on its Agriculture, Commerce, Laws Religion etc*. 1828; Sir Spenser St. John. *Hayti, or, the Black Republic*. 1889; William H. Ukers. *All About Coffee*. 1922; Michel-Rolph Trouillot. "Motion in the System: Coffee, Color, and Slavery in Eighteenth-Century Saint-Domingue." 1982; William Gervase, Clarence-Smith, and Steven Topik. *The Global Coffee Economy in Africa, Asia, and Latin America, 1500–1989*. Appendix: Historical Statistics of Coffee Production and Trade from 1700 to 1960. 2006; and USDA Foreign Agricultural Service: Production, Supply, and Distribution Online.

73. Simon Fass. *Political Economy in Haiti: The Drama of Survival*. 1988. p. 2.

74. Quotes from this paragraph come from: Franklin. *The Present State of Haiti (Saint Domingo), 1828: With Remarks on its Agriculture, Commerce, Laws Religion etc*. 1971. p. 11; Michel-Rolph Trouillot. *Haiti: State Against Nation*. 1990. p. 16; and Zora Neale Hurston. *Tell My Horse: Voodoo and Life in Haiti and Jamaica*. Chapter 7: The Next Hundred Years. 1938. Pétionville and Kenscoff are affluent Port-au-Prince suburbs, located in the mountains above the city.

75. William H. Ukers. *All About Coffee*. 1922. p. 8.

76. MINUSTAH. "Haïti: La Forêt des Pins, un patrimoine à sauvegarder." 2013.

77. Most coffee-growing countries have just one harvest per year. Some countries that are close to the equator and have multiple rainy seasons, like Colombia, have two harvests.

78. If only one seed develops inside a cherry it will be round like a pea. These are called peaberries. In some countries they're separated from all other beans and sell at a premium.

79. The coffee cherries of most commonly cultivated varieties turn red when ripe. A few varieties, however, become yellow, orange, or even pinkish when ripe.

80. Jean Nicolas Wintgens. *Coffee: Growing, Processing, Sustainable Production*. 2009. p. 616.

81. Thompson Owen. Sweet Maria's. "New(ish) Methods in Brazil Coffee Production."

82. World Bank. "Haiti Coffee Supply Chain: Risk Assessment." 2010; Ministere de l'Agriculture des Ressources Naturelles et du Developpement Rural, Institut National du Café d'Haïti, and Banque Interamericaine de Developpement. "Cadre Strategique de Developpement de la Filiere Cafe d'Haïti." 2011; and Institut National du Café d'Haïti. "Actualisation du diagnostic de la filière café en Haïti." Draft version. 2013.

83. People debate the idiosyncrasies of these terms and the coffees they describe. See "Confused? Naturally," by Chris Schooley of Coffee Shrub; and "A response to Chris Schooley's 'Confused? Naturally,'" by Peter Giuliano.

84. The female merchants are called *madam saras* in Haitian Creole. There are tens of thousands of them in Haiti, and they trade any and every type of produce. Most of them transport agricultural products from the countryside to sell in urban areas, and then transport dry or durable goods from the capital or D.R. border back to the countryside. I've heard that some of the *madam saras* at the very top of the Haiti-merchant pyramid now regularly fly to Panama, or even China, to trade. For more background, see Sidney W. Mintz. *Capital, saving and credit in peasant societies*. "The employment of capital by market women in Haiti." 1964; Mintz. *Boston Review*. "Remembering Haiti: Lessons from the field." March 1, 2010; and Talitha Stam. Cordaid. "From Gardens to Markets: A Madam Sara Perspective." 2012.

85. Willem J. Boot describes various coffee processing methods in *Roast Magazine*, "Wet, Dry, and Everything in Between: How coffee processing affects your cup (Part 1 of 2)." January/February 2007.

86. When it comes to green coffee, there are separate requirements for a coffee to make the specialty grade: a 350-gram sample must contain zero primary defects and no more than five secondary defects, as defined by the SCAA. See Specialty Coffee Association of America. Cupping Protocols; Green Coffee Grading Protocols.

87. Ukers. *All About Coffee*. 1922. p. 361.

88. Sir Spenser St. John was an unabashed racist, and contemporaries blasted his 1889 account, *Hayti or the Black Republic*, for its racism, sensationalizing of the Vodou religion, and wild tales of cannibalism. The coffee processing he describes, however, resembles the same practices you see in the Haitian countryside today, and Ukers reported a similar level of neglect in *All About Coffee*. 1922.

89. Christian A. Girault discusses traditional export markets in *Le commerce du café en Haïti: Habitants, spéculateurs et exportateurs*, 1981; as does Ukers in *All About Coffee*. 1922. K. Annabelle Smith writes about the New Orleans coffee market in *Smithsonian Magazine*, "The History of the Chicory Coffee Mix That New Orleans Made Its Own." March 5, 2014.

90. Marcelin Norvilus and Marie Ardys Jean Baptiste describe the *tchoka* coffee supply chain in "Etude des Filières Agricoles Haitiennes: Projet Appui au renforcement de la capacité des caisses du réseau de l'ANACAPH dans la réduction de la pauvreté en Haïti." Association Nationale des Caisses Populaires Haïtiennes. 2008. Discussion of honey processing draws from Willem J. Boot. *Roast Magazine*. "Fruity, Fermented, and Everything in Between: How coffee processing affects your cup (Part 2 of 2)." March/April 2007.

91. Oliver Strand. "Why Is Coffee in Paris So Bad?" *The New York Times Magazine*. April 8, 2010.

92. Interview with Jobert Angrand. May 2013.

93. Haiti's four major coffee areas are: Baptiste, in the Central Plateau; Beaumont, in the Grande Anse; Dondon, in the North; and Thiotte, in the Southeast.

94. Yams aren't actually a good complementary crop for coffee—left untended, the vines grow rampant and can smother coffee plants. But yams do often sell high on local markets.

95. Robert Fatton. *Haiti's Predatory Republic: The Unending Transition to Democracy*. 2002. p. xi.

96. One bag equals 60 kilograms of green coffee, about 132 pounds. USDA Foreign Agricultural Service: Production, Supply, and Distribution Online.

97. Background on pledged funding comes from the United Nations: "International Conference Raises Almost $10 Billion as More Than 130 Donors Contribute 'Towards a New Future for Haiti.'" March 31, 2010. Vijaya Ramachandran and Julie Walz, of the Center for Global Development, document spending in the two years that followed the disaster: "Haiti: Where Has All the Money Gone?" May 2012.

98. Marjorie Valbrun documented the drinking-water account for the Center for Public Integrity, "After the quake, praise becomes resentment in Haiti." January 10, 2012. Nestlé reported sending nearly 500,000 bottles of water to Haiti in the three weeks following the earthquake. "As Almost Half-Million Bottles Reach Haiti, Nestlé Waters North America Continues Work with Relief Agencies to Deliver Emergency Water." February 5, 2010. The company sent more than 3 million bottles in all. Nestlé Waters. Disaster Relief: Haiti earthquake relief.

99. For a detailed account of the response that followed the disaster, see Jonathan M. Katz's *The Big Truck That Went By: How the World Came to Save Haiti and Left Behind a Disaster*. 2014.

100. Center for Economic and Policy Research: Haiti Relief and Reconstruction Watch. "USAID's Disclosure of Local Partner Info Raises Troubling Questions." March 30, 2012. At the time, USAID awarded about 10 percent of its funding to local institutions worldwide. "USAID Forward Progress Report 2013." p. 14. For more background on USAID spending in the years following the earthquake see: "Haiti Reconstruction: USAID Infrastructure Projects Have Had Mixed Results and Face Sustainability Challenges." U.S. Government Accountability Office. June 2013.

101. Maura R. O'Connor reports on the post-quake coordination meetings at the U.N. base. "Does

International Aid Keep Haiti Poor?" *Slate*. January 7, 2011. Background on the U.N. agencies operating in Haiti at the time come from "Report of the United Nations in Haiti 2010: Situation, Challenges and Outlook," and from The United Nations Office for Project Services.

102. Laurent Dubois. *Haiti: The Aftershocks of History*. 2012. p. 174.

103. U.N. Office of the Special Envoy for Haiti. "Has aid Changed?: Channelling assistance to Haiti before and after the earthquake." 2011. p. 6, 30.

104. International Monetary Fund. "Haiti: Selected Issues. IMF Country Report No. 13/91." March 2013. p. 8.

105. Raoul Peck. *Assistance mortelle*. 2013.

106. Phone interview with Marc Eddy Martin. October 2013.

107. The origins of the *Code du Café* are documented by Diego Arias, Emily Brearly, and Gilles Damais. Inter-American Development Bank. "Restoring the Competitiveness of the Coffee Sector in Haiti." 2006. For background on coffee marketing in Haiti, see Christian A. Girault's *Le commerce du café en Haiti: Habitants, spéculateurs et exportateurs*. 1981; and Mats Lundahl with Yves Bourdet. *Politics or Markets? Essays on Haitian Underdevelopment*. "Haitian Coffee Marketing Revisited." 1992. Simon Fass also discusses various aspects of Haitian coffee marketing, noting that coffee growers received just 45-50 percent of export price, compared to the 60-75 percent that growers received when it came to commodities consumed domestically. *Political Economy in Haiti: The Drama of Survival*. 1988. p. 27.

108. Figures on 1980s exports come from the World Bank. "Haiti Agricultural Sector Review." 1991. Figures on 1955 exports come from Mats Lundahl. *Poverty in Haiti: Essays on Underdevelopment and Post Disaster Prospects*. 2010. p. 35.

109. Background on the series of coffee projects comes from: Samuel R. Daines. USAID. Practical Concepts Inc. "Impact Evaluation of the Haiti Small Farmer Improvement Project." 1979; Craig V. Olson, Steven C. Franzel, Kenneth E. Koehn, and Marc-Eddy Martin. USAID. Development Alternatives, Inc. "Evaluation of the Haiti Small Farmer Coffee Marketing Project." 1984; USAID. Private Enterprise and Agricultural Development Office. "Coffee Revitalization Project." 1994; Luke Dunnington and Tom Lenaghan. Development Alternatives, Inc. "A Case Study in Brand Creation with Small Holders: Haitian Bleu." 2006; and USAID. Market Chain Enhancement Project. "Coffee Sector Review and Proposed Coffee Action Plan." 2009.

110. Craig V. Olson et al. USAID. Development Alternatives, Inc. "Evaluation of the Haiti Small Farmer Coffee Marketing Project." 1984; and World Bank. "Haiti Agricultural Sector Review." 1991.

111. Interview with Michael Fairbanks. May 2013.

112. Background on the Rwandan coffee sector draws from Peterson Tumwebaze. "Coffee export revenues increase to over Rwf43b in November 2015." *The New Times*. January 12, 2016; John Spray. International Growth Centre. "How coffee can drive economic growth." February 18, 2015; Laura Fraser. "Coffee, and Hope, Grow in Rwanda." *The New York Times*. August 6, 2006; and USAID. Chemonics International Inc. "Rwanda Coffee Industry Value Chain Analysis: Profiling the actors, their interaction, costs, contracts and opportunities." 2010.

113. USAID. Private Enterprise and Agricultural Development Office. "Coffee Revitalization Project." 1994.

114. H. Art Schar, Rolando Vasquez M., and Kenneth D. Weiss. USAID. LAC TECH Project. "Evaluation of the Coffee Revitalization Project." 1994.

115. Background on these projects comes from TechnoServe: "The Coffee Initiative: Phase One Final Report: 2008 to 2011." 2013; and "The Coffee Initiative: Lessons Learned." 2013.

116. Craig V. Olson et al. USAID. Development Alternatives, Inc. "Evaluation of the Haiti Small Farmer Coffee Marketing Project." 1984.

117. International Trade Centre. Trade Map. Haiti and Rwanda Data.

118. Data from World Bank. "Haiti Agricultural Sector Review." 1991; and International Trade Centre. Trade Map. Haiti Data.

119. Usually, somewhere between 20 and 40 coffees qualify for the Cup of Excellence competition, depending upon the country and the year. In Honduras in 2015, nine out of the 38 Cup of Excellence coffees sold for $4.50 per pound or less. The top coffees often sell for $20 per pound, or sometimes much higher. See: the Alliance for Coffee Excellence: Cup of Excellence.

120. Thompson Owen. Sweet Maria's. "How To Buy Full Bags of Coffee...or not." 2004.

121. Phone interview with Chris Wade. December 2013. A report by Tom Lenaghan notes that Coffee Bean International bought Haitian coffee at the time: Development Alternatives, Inc. DAIdeas. "Haitian Bleu: A Rare Taste of Success For Haiti's Coffee Farmers." December 2005.

122. Philippe Thoby-Marcelin and Pierre Marcelin. *The Beast of the Haitian Hills*. 1946. p. xix.

123. For a detailed account of the beginnings of direct trade, see Michaele Weissman's *God in a Cup: The Obsessive Quest for the Perfect Coffee*. 2008. When it comes to fair trade, examples of these organizations include Fairtrade International, Fair Trade USA, and Max Havelaar Fairtrade Netherlands, among others. Kerry Howley outlined fair trade's roots in *Reason Magazine*, "Absolution in Your Cup: The real meaning of Fair Trade coffee." March 2006.

124. Some past USAID coffee projects encouraged and assisted Haitian co-ops to become fair-trade certified. But for coffee farmers in Haiti, the certification and auditing fees that farmer groups have to pay the third-party organizations can be a big hindrance. These fees are often a few thousand dollars for initial certification and a few hundred dollars for subsequent yearly audits. The costs aren't a big deal for many cooperatives in countries that have high levels of production. But because Haitian farmer groups produce such low volumes, they wind up spreading those fees across meager quantities of coffee. The relative costs can end up being so high that some Haitian cooperatives have purposefully let their fair-trade certifications lapse.

125. In fact, fair-trade-labeled coffee might be expected to fall in quality over time, because farmers with poor-quality coffee could be tempted to certify as a way to increase revenues without having to produce better coffee.

126. Raluca Dragusanu, Daniele Giovannucci, and Nathan Nunn discuss fair trade requirements in "The Economics of Fair Trade." *Journal of Economic Perspectives*. 2014. USDA describes organic requirements in "What is Organic Certification?" National Organic Program. Agricultural Marketing Service. June 2012.

127. For examples of supply-chain projects, see "Fair Trade USA 2014 Almanac" and "Fair Trade USA 2013 Annual Report."

128. Kim Elena Ionescu. Specialty Coffee Association of America Symposium. "Mo' Money, Mo' Quality, and other Myths about Microlots." 2013.

129. Hannah Popish and Kim Elena Ionescu. Counter Culture Coffee. "The Social Impact of Microlots: A Coffee Cooperative Case Study in Ihuamaca, Peru." March 2012.

130. Ruth Ann Church, Hannah Popish, and Kim Elena Ionescu. Michigan State University Deptartment of Community Sustainability and Counter Culture Coffee, with Virmax Café. "Impact of Microlot Premiums on Smallholder Coffee Producers in Southern Colombia: How Premiums Are Invested and Farming Practices Employed." December 2013.

131. Craig V. Olson et al. USAID. Development Alternatives, Inc. "Evaluation of the Haiti Small Farmer Coffee Marketing Project." 1984.

132. Background on the TechnoServe initiatives comes from two of the organization's reports: "The Coffee Initiative: Phase One Final Report: 2008 to 2011." 2013; and "The Coffee Initiative: Lessons Learned." 2013.

133. La Colombe. "Savan Zombi: A Sourcing Story." August 20, 2015.

134. As cited by Laurent Dubois in *Haiti: The Aftershocks of History*. 2012. p. 165. Originally from Joseph-Anténor Firmin. *M. Roosevelt, président des États-Unis et la République d'Haïti*. p. 463.

135. According to World Bank data on mobile cellular subscriptions.

136. Raju Jan Singh and Mary Barton-Dock. World Bank. "Haiti—Toward a new narrative: systematic

country diagnostic." 2015. p. 19.

137. Data on aid given to Haiti come from USAID Greenbook. Economic Analysis and Data Services. U.S. Overseas Loans and Grants: Obligations and Loan Authorizations, July 1, 1945-September 30, 2013. Stephanie Hanes notes how Duvalier pocketed aid in "Jean-Claude Duvalier, ex-Haitian leader known as Baby Doc, dies at 63." *The Washington Post.* October 4, 2014. Siri Schubert noted aid funds stolen by Duvalier in "Haiti: The Long Road to Recovery: Public money stolen by a corrupt president finally to be returned." *Frontline.* May 22, 2009.

138. For an overview on where and why aid is spent, see "Misplaced charity: Aid is best spent in poor, well-governed countries. That isn't where it goes." *The Economist.* June 11, 2016. Recent data from the OECD also suggest that when it comes to aid per person living in extreme poverty, the poorest and least-developed countries receive less aid than relatively better-off ones do. See Marcus Manuel. "Getting to zero poverty by 2030—stop giving more to those that need it the least." Development Progress. October 7, 2014. For more background on top U.S. aid recipients and underlying motivations for giving aid, see Helen V. Milner and Dustin H. Tingley. "The Political Economy of U.S. Foreign Aid: American Legislators and the Domestic Politics of Aid." *Economics & Politics.* 2010.

139. "Overview of U.S. Policy Towards Haiti Prior To The Elections." U.S. Senate Foreign Relations Committee. Subcommittee on Western Hemisphere, Transnational Crime, Civilian Security, Democracy, Human Rights, And Global Women's Issues. July 15, 2015.

140. William J. Clinton. "Address to the Nation on Haiti." September 15, 1994.

141. For detail about aid to Haiti during this period, see USAID's report, "Providing Emergency Aid to Haiti." 1999; and USAID Greenbook. Economic Analysis and Data Services. U.S. Overseas Loans and Grants: Obligations and Loan Authorizations, July 1, 1945-September 30, 2013.

142. Three recent scientific papers discuss potential effects of climate change on coffee: Christian Bunn, Peter Läderach, Oriana Ovalle Rivera, and Dieter Kirschke. "A bitter cup: Climate change profile of global production of Arabica and Robusta coffee." *Climatic Change.* 2014; Oriana Ovalle-Rivera, Peter Läderach, Christian Bunn, Michael Obersteiner, and Götz Schroth. International Center for Tropical Agriculture. "Projected Shifts in Coffea arabica Suitability among Major Global Producing Regions Due to Climate Change." 2015; and Christian Bunn, Peter Läderach, Juan Guillermo Pérez Jimenez, Christophe Montagnon, and Timothy Schilling. International Center for Tropical Agriculture. "Multiclass Classification of Agro-Ecological Zones for Arabica Coffee: An Improved Understanding of the Impacts of Climate Change." 2015. Haiti's coffee-growing area is also expected to shrink by 2050, especially in the lower-altitude northern mountains, while mango and cacao may become more viable.

Anton Eitzinger, Peter Läderach, Stephania Carmona, Laure Collet, Ludger Jean-Simon, Patricia Dufane, and Andreea Nowak. International Center for Tropical Agriculture. "Haiti: Coffee and Mango Production in a Changing Climate." 2014.

143. International Coffee Organization. "Sustainability of the coffee sector in Africa." 2015.

144. Market data and detail on specialty coffee's growth come from USDA Foreign Agricultural Service: Production, Supply, and Distribution Online; and Specialty Coffee Association of America. U.S. Specialty Coffee Facts & Figures. December 2015. Karen Stabiner reported on specialty's rise in Europe in *The Wall Street Journal*, "Europe (Finally) Wakes Up to Superior Coffee," September 29, 2015; as did Nicholas Bariyo and Alexandra Wexler. *The Wall Street Journal.* "Specialty Coffee Heats Up in Africa." February 5, 2016. Sophia Yan reported on Starbucks' plan to open cafes in China for *CNN Money.* "Starbucks adding 1,400 new shops in China." January 12, 2016.

145. Nicholas Bariyo and Alexandra Wexler. *The Wall Street Journal.* "Specialty Coffee Heats Up in Africa." February 5, 2016.

146. Per capita income data for Haiti and Colombia come from the World Bank. The USDA Foreign Agricultural Service's "Coffee: World Markets and Trade" documented Colombia's coffee consumption practices. December 2015.

147. The relatively high local coffee prices in Haiti may not last much longer. In early 2016, the

government announced that the two largest local roasters received permits to import 20,000 bags of green coffee from Uganda and Vietnam, at about $1.27 per pound, significantly lower than prices on local markets that crop year. *Le Nouvelliste*. "Haïti conduite à importer du café vert." March 31, 2016.

www.ingramcontent.com/pod-product-compliance
Lightning Source LLC
Chambersburg PA
CBHW050501290526
45786CB00006B/2391